'A story of sheer political grit, courage and conviction, proving that even in the darkest hour there remain people loyal to their principles.'
South African Deputy President Kgalema Motlanthe

'The new insights that Robin Renwick brings to the extraordinary life and achievements of the late Helen Suzman will help to ensure that this exceptional South African and universally acknowledged human rights campaigner is accorded her rightful place in history.'
John Battersby, former editor of the *Sunday Independent*

'An admirable and affectionate portrait of a remarkable woman.'
David Welsh, author of *The Rise and Fall of Apartheid*

'A remarkable biography about a memorable woman. As British ambassador to South Africa, Lord Robin Renwick established a lasting friendship with Helen Suzman. Hence the excellence of this biography: the clarity of language, grasp and depth of issues, the human touch that pervades every chapter, and the deceptively easy readability. Coming at a time when liberalism has again come to the forefront of the national debate, it could not have appeared at a better moment.'
Stanley Uys, veteran South African journalist and political commentator

'Helen Suzman was sharp, incisive, principled and loads of fun. So's this biography by Robin Renwick.'
John Carlin, journalist and author of *Invictus*

HELEN SUZMAN

THE BIOGRAPHY

HELEN SUZMAN

Bright Star in a Dark Chamber

ROBIN RENWICK

Biteback Publishing

First published in South Africa in 2014 by Jonathan Ball Publishers

Copyright © in published edition: Jonathan Ball Publishers,
South Africa

This edition published by Biteback Publishing Ltd
Westminster Tower
3 Albert Embankment
London SE1 7SP
Copyright © Robin Renwick 2014

ISBN 978-184954-667-6

10 9 8 7 6 5 4 3 2 1

A CIP catalogue record for this book is available from the British Library.

Set in Minion

Printed and bound in Great Britain by
CPI Group (UK) Ltd, Croydon CR0 4YY

Contents

Chapter X

If she could speak truth to power then, when
it was so dangerous, we must do so now

Appendix

Notes

Acknowledgements

Introduction

Like everybody else, I long to be loved.
But I am not prepared to make any
concessions whatsoever
Helen Suzman

Ever since I started taking an interest in South African affairs – an interest that began when I was an undergraduate at Cambridge, where earnest progressives sought to establish their anti-apartheid credentials by declining to drink South African sherry – the activities of Helen Suzman always seemed to me to offer the clearest beacon of hope that some kind of sanity might in the end prevail.

When, nearly 30 years later, I arrived in South

Africa as a fledgling British ambassador, I still had never met this woman I so much admired. I did so with some trepidation. In the course of her political career Mrs Suzman had seen a great many high commissioners, and then ambassadors, come and go, some I am sure more memorable than others. Yet I was greeted with all the friendliness and helpfulness that had been shown to every one of my predecessors and the innumerable other well-intentioned foreigners who regarded Helen Suzman as their most reliable guide to the political labyrinth of apartheid.

I was delighted to find that, in addition to being the most determined and effective opponent of injustice, Helen Suzman also was the most entertaining company it was possible to find in South Africa, or anywhere else for that matter. However difficult the circumstances, lunch with her was sure to end in gales of laughter, and I will never again be able to watch anyone pouring soda into a glass of whisky without hearing Helen say: 'Don't drown it!'

Never lacking in resourcefulness, on one well-remembered occasion, trying to avoid violence at a demonstration in Cape Town, she was confronted by a snarling Alsatian police dog straining on its leash to get at her. A dog-lover herself, she ordered the animal to sit, which it proceeded meekly to do, convulsing even the police with laughter at their own expense.

In the course of weekend fishing trips with her in the eastern Transvaal I discovered that, as in her dealings with her political opponents, she did not believe in taking any prisoners. Every trout she caught was dispatched to the smokery and served up for future dinners, while I was painstakingly returning mine to the river from which they came.

Behind the clear blue eyes, sparkling with intelligence, lay a biting wit, steely resolve and utter determination never to let up in her attacks on the system she abhorred until she saw it crumbling around her. Over four decades, she campaigned relentlessly against every manifestation of apartheid – against grand apartheid and petty apartheid, forced removals and the homelands policy, detention without trial and all abuses of authority on behalf of the victims and countless millions disenfranchised by the system.

This book recalls the determination, indeed ferocity, with which she opposed every one of the apartheid laws and the spate of security legislation introduced by the Verwoerd and Vorster governments. In the elections of October 1961, Mrs Suzman was the only representative of the Progressive Party to be elected. Thereafter, she had to carry on a lone battle in parliament for the next 13 years. The greatest burden, she once said, was 'the fear that I won't come up to expectations. So many people depend on my acquitting myself well.'[1]

She had to face the hostility not only of the government but also of her own former party, one of whose spokesmen accused Helen Suzman of 'having nothing but a lot of principles she waffles about'. The first part of the accusation undoubtedly was true, but, as the reader of these pages will discover, Helen Suzman was never known to waffle.

In 1969, in response to fresh security legislation enacted by the government, she declared: 'There is another interpretation to violence, apart from the violence against the state ... violence can also mean the unfettered use of power by the state against a citizen, so as to deprive him of his normal civil rights. In this sense we have seen a great deal of violence in South Africa. Mass removals of African people from their homes is a violence ... Banning, house arrests, detention without trial, banishment are all a violence.'[2]

In every succeeding year, she continued to campaign grimly on behalf of the detainees, asking what the government proposed to do with these people who had not been tried for any crime. Did it intend to keep them locked up for life? They were certainly not going to alter their political views as a result of being detained.

There was no principle that mattered more to her than the rule of law: 'I believe that when liberal values and the rule of law are abandoned, the slide away from simple justice and fair play towards despotism and dirty tricks is a swift slide indeed.'[3]

Her career in politics was marked by a degree of intellectual rigour and honesty rare among political figures. To some people's dismay, she insisted on acknowledging positive change when it did, eventually, take place – generally in the form of the government recognising belatedly the force of arguments she had deployed over the past 20 years. The scrapping of the pass laws, the repeal of the prohibition of mixed marriages, the legalisation of black trade unions and the ending of job reservation – she recognised all these as real reforms. But in 1983 she showed herself as implacably determined as ever in opposing the tricameral constitution, under which separate legislatures were created for the Indian and coloured communities to deal with their 'own affairs'.

Helen Suzman, once again, was swimming against the tide. The new constitution was approved by a large majority in the referendum of white voters. The black majority were not consulted and their exclusion led to the wave of violence in the townships from 1984 to 1986, which, in turn, triggered the states of emergency and the intensification of sanctions against South Africa.

Helen Suzman cared passionately about South Africa's international position and reputation, reflecting her profound conviction that self-inflicted isolation could lead only to political and economic disaster. She constantly was accused of being 'unpatriotic', though no one who knew her could think of any more ludicrous charge. Accused of asking questions to embarrass South Africa abroad, she declared: 'It is not my questions that embarrass South Africa: it is your answers!'[4]

She described her principal opponents in parliament – Verwoerd, John Vorster and PW Botha – as being 'as nasty a trio as you could encounter in your worst nightmares'. On being told by Verwoerd that he had written her off, her response was: 'And the whole world has written you off.' When PW Botha observed in parliament that she did not like him, she responded: 'Like you? I cannot stand you!'[5] On another occasion she purred: 'I do not know why we equate – and with the examples before us – a white skin with civilisation!'[6]

When we reread these exchanges, it is easy to forget just how formidable, ruthless and forbidding these people were. Her speeches in parliament were subject to constant heckling, much of it not recorded in Hansard, leading to such exchanges as: 'On a point of order, may an Hon. Member call me a Communist?' Mr PJ Coetzee: 'I said she was almost a Communist.' Rounding on one of her constant interrupters, she said: 'The Hon. Member has not moved out of Rustenburg to the best of my knowledge, but of course he is an expert on the world scene. Let him stand up and make a speech instead of muttering at my back. It will be a welcome change.'[7]

This is the story not just of one remarkable woman, but of a whole legion of people who, often from very different perspectives, were engaged in the struggle against apartheid but who, in many cases, owed a great deal to her efforts to help them. John Vorster accused Helen Suzman of permitting herself to be used. This was an allegation she never really sought to deny because she was indeed ready to defend the rights and liberties of people, some of whom would not have been prepared to accord her any rights or liberties at all. As the champion of all those who were detained or imprisoned for their political views, she made representations on behalf of virtually the entire leadership of the South African Communist Party (SACP), as well as of the African National Congress (ANC) and the Pan Africanist Congress (PAC), seeking not only to get them released but also to have their prison conditions improved, to have their relatives enabled to visit them and a chance for them to pursue their studies by correspondence, especially through the University of South Africa (Unisa). The countless tributes to her in the archive bear witness to the practical improvements she achieved for prisoners and detainees, as well as to her untiring efforts to accelerate their release.

It is not possible in politics to succeed without a certain amount of steel in one's character. Helen Suzman devoted her political career to the pursuit of high principles. But, as the lone progressive voice in the parliaments of Verwoerd and Vorster, she most certainly would not have succeeded in making herself heard without a quite formidable display of fighting qualities. She was not prepared to be silenced or bullied or intimidated, nor was she ever prepared to suffer fools gladly. Indeed she showed a total incapacity to suffer fools at all. In the words of her close friend and cousin, Irene Menell: 'Those who know her will confirm that personal tolerance is not one of her strongest characteristics and yet she has never failed to defend the rights of those with whom she disagrees.'[8]

Why was she so effective in fighting for the causes in which she believed? She never believed that, to influence the authorities, it was sufficient to issue a statement deploring or condemning what they were doing. When, on my own arrival in South Africa, I went to remonstrate with a South African minister about the tribulations of the Magopa people, victims of forced removal, he said: 'Oh no! I have just had the most dreadful hour with Mrs Suzman about the Magopa people – and now there is you!' In the end something – though not enough – *was* done for the Magopas.[9] But Helen Suzman always tried to tackle those responsible directly, to try to make them think again and correct the damage they had done. When that tactic failed, as it often did, she would appeal to the South African and world press.

But, temperamentally, she did not believe in

posturing; she believed in trying to get results. When the authorities threatened, in response to the rent boycott, to cut off power to large areas of Soweto in midwinter, it was Helen Suzman who persuaded the Administrator of the Transvaal of the folly of such a course.

Helen Suzman remarked that one of the greatest ironies for her, towards the end of her 36 years in the South African parliament, was to sit in the House of Assembly listening to speeches by National Party ministers, addressed to their right-wing opponents, that might have been made by her 20 years before. On the 40th anniversary of National Party rule, she suggested that there wasn't much to celebrate: the best she could find to say was that, over the past ten years, the government had replaced some of the laws it should never have put on the statute book in the first place. For, under the pressure of the economic laws and moral compulsions to which she constantly drew attention, and in response to her own relentless logic, the government had come to acknowledge that most – though in their minds not yet all – features of the apartheid system simply would not work.

Unlike those who appeared to be waiting for the attainment of the millennium, Helen Suzman knew, and constantly said, that the problems for the black majority would not end when they took their rightful place in government. For that reason, and because of her wider experience of the rest of the world, she was deeply concerned about the conditions, and particularly the economic conditions, under which 'liberation' eventually would be achieved. It was not going to be of enormous help to the people of South Africa for a white ruling class to be replaced by a black ruling class in circumstances in which the population increase and economic decline meant that no government could hope to preside over anything other than steadily worsening circumstances for the population at large. 'Liberation' in many African countries had turned out to be a bitter experience once majority rule had been achieved.

As a result, Helen Suzman never was prepared to support the campaigns for general sanctions and disinvestment. She noted that, particularly in the United States, disinvestment had become the popular solution. She could understand the appeal of such a course as a moral stand based on the idea of disassociation from the abhorrent system of apartheid and of keeping one's hands clean. But, in her view, the effect of disinvestment was symbolic, and it removed what influence US business had on the course of events. She refused to support measures like the proposed ban on South Africa's agricultural exports, which would have cost tens of thousands of black and coloured workers their jobs, in the absence of any alternative employment or any social safety net.

She was no more prepared to bow to the prevailing wind on these subjects than she was to make any concessions whatever over human rights. Because she believed that, far from encouraging further reform, the worst features of the system would be accentuated if the country were pushed into a state of siege, she constantly fought against South Africa's isolation.

The academic and cultural boycotts she regarded as particularly self-defeating, as they penalised the liberal English-speaking universities: 'Those who believe in the cultural boycott,' she said, 'think they are on the side of the angels. In fact they are on the side of the idiots.' She was delighted in 1988 that her niece, the actress Janet Suzman, ignored the boycott, directing a white actress as Desdemona opposite a black South African Othello, John Kani, at the Market Theatre in Johannesburg, causing a small sensation given that, until two years before, sex across the colour line had been banned in South Africa.

Her stand on these issues brought her criticism from others engaged in the struggle against apartheid, but she was no more prepared to accept intolerance or attempts to censor her views and make her toe the party line from the left than she was from the right.

Her independence of spirit was, in my view, the most important of all the examples Helen Suzman has set us. She was conscious that there were two kinds of critics of censorship: those who genuinely believed that the press must be free and remain so, and those who objected to censorship by the regime, while looking forward to the day when they might exercise it themselves.

She continued her fight to try to ensure that the struggle against apartheid ended in success – but in circumstances that offered some hope that the values for which she had fought so valiantly would be observed better in the future than they had been in the past. In that respect she was indeed a 'hard' rather than a 'soft' liberal, because what she believed in was not a tactical progressive stance but the defence of liberalism itself, which had to be protected against all comers.

In one of her last speeches in the South African parliament, in May 1989, she declared:

> I have to admit, without actually saying 'I told
> you so', that it has been a source of considerable
> satisfaction to me … to have been present in Par-
> liament when many of the laws which I opposed
> when they were introduced have since been re-
> pealed, years later in most cases …[10]

Her final intervention in parliament took the form, characteristically, of an attempt to censure a judge for the derisory sentence imposed on two white farmers who beat to death a black man who had caused the death of one of their dogs.

What, then, did Helen Suzman's influence mean? Internally, it helped to move even her political opponents towards a realisation that the policies to which they were committed were unworkable and would have to be abandoned. For her arguments, always marshalled with great skill and expressed in her own characteristically vivid fashion, were in the end unanswerable.

Externally, she had a fundamental effect on the way in which people in Britain and in other Western countries viewed South Africa. The example she set, and the campaign she waged, served to keep the flag of decency flying and, in doing so, to demonstrate to millions of black South Africans that she and many other white South Africans were prepared to fight against the injustices they were suffering and were genuinely committed to a future non-racial society in which all South Africans must have equal rights. And on the extent to which the values she defended while the majority were oppressed are defended also when they are in power will depend the chances for a successful post-apartheid society in South Africa.

The last word on this subject should rest with Helen herself: 'Like everybody else, I long to be loved. But I am not prepared to make any concessions whatsoever.'

Chapter 1

*And when he was dead, did you still
think he was shamming?*

On 25 September 1977 a large, angry and hostile
crowd of black South Africans gathered on the out-
skirts of King William's Town in the east of the Cape
Province for the funeral of Steve Biko.

Biko had been an organiser for the all-black South
African Students' Organisation (SASO). He became
the leading spokesman of the Black Conscious-
ness Movement (BCM), according to which black
people had first to get rid of the mental servitude
that had developed among them. They must look to

themselves for their own salvation. This was a more radical doctrine than that of the ANC, and, with the charismatic young Steve Biko at its head, the movement rapidly developed a large following among the region's desperately poor townships.

Biko's close friend Donald Woods, the leading newspaper editor in the region, had contacted Helen Suzman to arrange for Steve Biko to meet her during a visit he was planning to make to Cape Town. En route to Cape Town by car, Biko and a coloured friend, Peter Jones, were stopped and detained by the police. On 6 September he was taken by the security police to Port Elizabeth, where he was interrogated for 48 hours. He then was transferred to Pretoria Central prison, over 1,100km away, in the back of a Land Rover. He died in the prison hospital on 12 September, aged 30. Dr Jonathan Gluckman, called in by Biko's family to conduct a postmortem, telephoned Helen Suzman. 'Helen, they murdered him,' he said.

At the subsequent inquest, much of which she attended, the great advocate Sydney Kentridge cross-examined one of the security policemen who had been a member of the interrogation team. Kentridge asked whether he had thought Biko was shamming injuries during his brutal interrogation. 'Yes, your worship,' was the reply. Kentridge asked the security policeman whether he thought Biko still was shamming when he found him sitting fully clothed in a bathtub full of water. 'Yes,' he replied. When Kentridge asked, once Biko was dead, did he still think he was shamming, 'Yes, your worship,' was the reply.

The inquest came after the funeral. But none of the tens of thousands of mainly young, male, black South Africans attending that event had any doubt what had happened to Steve Biko. Helen Suzman attended the funeral with two of her Progressive Party colleagues, Alex Boraine and Zach de Beer. The field was sodden. As they tried to make their way toward the podium through the huge crowd, their passage was barred by a group of young men, one of whom told them in a very hostile manner: 'We don't want you whites here.' Helen said that they had come to pay their respects to Steve Biko, but was told that she should go and talk to Vorster and Jimmy Kruger (the Minister of Justice, who infamously stated that Biko's death 'left him cold').

As the crowd hemmed them in, she became angry. 'I'm Helen Suzman,' she said, 'and I've come to pay my respects to Steve Biko.'

'Who did you say you are?' was the response.

'I'm Helen Suzman.'

'You prove that.'

With difficulty, she managed to open her handbag and extract a credit card. At this she was told, 'Mrs Suzman, I beg your pardon. You may certainly go through.' The crowd parted, causing Zach de Beer to say: 'Now I have seen everything!'

They reached the podium, which promptly collapsed. But they then witnessed an immensely impressive ceremony, with 20,000 black South Africans 'singing their heads off' in a spectacular display of sorrow and resistance.[1]

* * *

To Helen Suzman's fury, the magistrate presiding at the inquest, MJ Prins, refused to attribute any blame to the security police for Biko's death, though the evidence clearly showed that he had been struck on the head, causing extensive brain damage. In parliament she laid the responsibility squarely at the feet of Minister Kruger, saying of Steve Biko that he had been kept without clothing for days on end, in handcuffs and leg irons and, when already gravely ill, was transported unconscious in the back of a Land Rover for over 1,000 kilometres to Pretoria. The officer in charge, Colonel Piet Goosen, had told the inquest that the security police did not operate under any statutes. They were a law unto themselves.

As for Kruger, he first stated that Biko had died of a hunger strike and that it was a man's democratic right to starve himself to death. He then had changed his story to say that 'heads may roll', but none did. He was told by Mrs Suzman in full parliament that he would carry to his grave the infamy of his statement that Biko's death 'leaves me cold'.

Donald Woods was subjected to a banning order, rendering it impossible for him to publish his impassioned articles about the circumstances of his friend's death. He and his family left South Africa in a dramatic escape, later chronicled, with the story of Steve Biko, in Richard Attenborough's 1987 film, *Cry Freedom*.

Characteristically, Helen Suzman did not forget about Peter Jones, who had been arrested with Biko. In a bravura performance in parliament, she ended her speech about Steve Biko to dramatic effect by asking what had happened to Peter Jones. Where is Peter Jones? Why is he not being charged? And *how* is Peter Jones?[2] Her efforts succeeded, as Peter Jones was released, whereupon she helped to find him a job.

She considered that the two doctors who had visited Steve Biko in detention and failed to help him deserved 'especially dishonourable mention', supporting friends in the medical profession who succeeded, through a court case, in getting one of them, Dr Benjamin Tucker, struck off the medical register for six years.[3]

She also had befriended and exerted herself to help protect Biko's partner and mother of his child, Dr Mamphela Ramphele, at the time one of the few black woman doctors in South Africa. Dr Ramphele subsequently was banned and restricted to Tzaneen in the far north of the country, as far away as possible from King William's Town. Fifteen years later, after visiting the desperately impoverished township of Lenyenye near Tzaneen, Helen Suzman wrote in the Johannesburg *Sunday Times* that the only bright spot there was Dr Ramphele, who was running a medical and community service for the district on a shoestring. Despite the circumstances, Suzman found her radiating energy and good humour.[4]

Mamphela Ramphele was to serve with distinction in the new South Africa as vice-chancellor of the

University of Cape Town and with the World Bank, before giving up her position as chairperson of Gold Fields to become a forceful critic of the ruling ANC, founding her own opposition party, Agang SA.

Chapter II

He regarded her as a troublemaker

Helen Suzman was born in the mining town of Germiston just outside Johannesburg on 7 November 1917, the day of the Bolshevik Revolution in Russia. In later life it was to be a source of great satisfaction to her that she managed to outlive the three ideologies she abhorred as having inflicted untold misery on tens of millions of human beings in the succeeding decades – Nazism, communism and apartheid.

She was born into a family of recent immigrants from Lithuania. In 1905, in the village of Klykoliai in

Lithuania, then part of the Russian empire, the tsarist authorities had sought to levy a fine on the Gavronsky family because her father, Samuel, had failed to report for military service. Jewish families like the Gavronskys suffered various forms of discrimination, including a prohibition on joining any of the professions, and also were subject to periodic attacks or pogroms. Samuel Gavronsky followed his brother Oscar on the long sea voyage to South Africa and found in Johannesburg, centre of the gold mining industry, a town full of migrants looking to make their fortunes.

The Gavronskys were to form part of the extraordinary story of the Johannesburg Jewish community, never much more than 100,000 strong, yet which played an immensely influential role in the South African economy. The Oppenheimers, Hersovs and Menells came to dominate much of the mining industry. A high proportion of the Jewish immigrants came from Lithuania. The tsarist authorities, through their discriminatory policies, did much to accelerate the development of the South African economy.

The Gavronsky brothers knew nothing about mining and concentrated on supplying the miners, dealing in cattle, leather, clothing and real estate. The brothers married two sisters, also from Lithuania, Frieda and Hansa David.

When Helen Gavronsky was just two weeks old, her mother, Frieda, died, aged 28. Helen, her father and elder sister moved in with Oscar Gavronsky and his wife. Helen experienced no deprivation, but the loss of her mother before she had even known her probably did contribute to her fierce spirit of independence.

Her father, who had arrived in South Africa penniless at the age of 17, had little formal education, and there was scarcely a book in the house. He was too busy trying to make a living to have much time for anything else. He never spoke to her about her mother, she presumed because it was too painful a subject for him. She never saw a photograph of her mother until she was 55 years old.

When she was nine, her father got remarried, to an English-born divorcée named Debbie. Helen Suzman got on well with her stepmother, whom she described as a thoroughly nice woman, generous, hospitable and sociable. The upwardly mobile Gavronskys moved to a house built by Sir Herbert Baker in the expensive suburb of Parktown.

For her education, Helen was sent to the best school available, which was the Roman Catholic Parktown Convent. Many of the other private schools at the time did not take Jewish children. There she discovered a well-stocked library and developed a passionate appetite for reading. She was, she said, taught to learn by rote, which helped to give her an excellent memory. She also developed a love of sports. On the hockey pitch, the nuns taught her to be a bad loser, which, she contended, was good preparation for a career in politics. She grew up in an English-speaking Jewish Johannesburg environment in which Afrikaners figured very little, and with no contact with black South Africans other than the domestic staff at home and at the convent.

Having matriculated at 16, she started studying for a Bachelor of Commerce degree at the University of the Witwatersrand, but spent much of her time playing tennis and golf, swimming and dancing, which, together with the fact that she detested the accountancy course, led to failure in her third-year exams. She went, she claimed, to every single university dance. Her father had paid for her to make two trips to Europe on the Union-Castle shipping line. She wanted to stay in London and take her degree there at the London School of Economics, but Samuel insisted that she return to South Africa.

Helen did not feel that her education by the nuns had any particular influence on her views on race relations, and her self-made father, with whom she got on well, despite having little in common with him, was no liberal at all. They had, she said, many an argument about politics and race relations. He could never really understand why she bothered about the conditions of the black population. He did not try to dissuade her from entering parliament, but, once she had done so, in the course of an overseas trip, she learned that he had donated £500 to Dr Verwoerd's scholarship fund. She was met at the airport by her stepmother. 'Where is the old boy?' she inquired. 'Too scared to come,' was the reply. Congratulating her father on his generosity to her arch-enemy the prime minister, she suggested that he should donate the same amount to the Progressive Party, which he meekly agreed to do. She acknowledged inheriting from her father his stamina, love of animals and enjoyment of a glass of Scotch and soda in the evening.

In 1937, at the age of 19, she married Moses (Mosie) Suzman. Nearly 14 years her senior, he already was an eminent physician. They enjoyed dancing and horse riding. Their elder daughter, Frances, was born on 30 September 1939, shortly after the start of the Second World War. Helen then attempted to join the Women's Auxiliary Force, but was annoyed to be told instead to go home and look after her child. She returned to Wits University and within a year graduated with first-class honours. She got a humdrum job at the War Supplies Board, attempting to track down war profiteers.

Mosie Suzman joined the South African Medical Corps. Their second child, Patricia, was born after he had left to become second-in-command of the South African army hospital in Egypt. At the end of the war, the Suzmans built a large and rambling house, which they called Blue Haze, on a beautiful plot on what was then the northern edge of Johannesburg. There was as yet no reason to believe that this highly intelligent, happily married mother of two young children would make any particular impact on South African politics at all.[1]

* * *

The war ended, Helen Suzman was offered and accepted a tutorship, which later became a lectureship, in Economic History at Wits University, by

Professor Herbert Frankel, later Professor of Economics at Nuffield College, Oxford. Among the students who attended her lectures were Derek Keys, who later became finance minister in the De Klerk and Mandela governments, Mark Weinberg, Sydney Lipworth, Joe Slovo (later to become head of the SACP) and Eduardo Mondlane, who went on to lead the resistance movement (Frelimo) fighting Portuguese rule in Mozambique. Years later, meeting Mondlane at a conference in the US, she reminded him that he had written the best essay she had seen on the poor-white problem in South Africa. Asked about his plans, he intended, he said, to go back to drive the Portuguese out of Mozambique. After that, he planned to drive the whites out of South Africa, too. 'Not so easy,' was her reply. In 1969 Mondlane was killed in a letter-bomb explosion in Tanzania.

It was through her studies and lectures at the university that Helen Suzman became deeply interested in the migrant labour system on which the South African economy was based. In 1946 the prime minister, General Jan Smuts, had appointed the Native Laws Commission, also known as the Fagan Commission, to look into the problems raised by the massive wartime influx of hundreds of thousands of black workers into the urban areas. The pass laws, which hitherto had restricted the ability of blacks to move from the rural areas, had been suspended for the duration of the war.

As Helen Suzman said of him, Smuts was no liberal, but he was a man of considerable intellect. He understood that the migrant worker conditions that had applied to black South Africans before the war could hardly apply thereafter. As more and more Africans poured into the cities to work, efforts to stop this had failed. 'You might as well try to sweep back the ocean with a broom,' Smuts had declared.

The South African Institute of Race Relations (SAIRR) asked her to work on evidence to submit to the commission and sent her to participate in a conference on human rights in London in 1947. In a statement to the conference, she said:

> South Africa has a multiracial society, dominated … by a minority group determined to maintain its supremacy. While the spirit of trusteeship is supposed to be the basis of policy, it is a trusteeship which operates on the assumption that the ward will never be of age … The primitive state of the rural African is not well understood by

people living outside South Africa, while the rapid development of the urban native is not comprehended by people living in South Africa. There then is our problem – guidance rather than criticism is urgently needed.[2]

On her return to South Africa, she told the *Star* newspaper that delegates from other countries did not realise 'the South African rural native's extreme primitiveness, both in his mentality and his living conditions, and the difficulty at this juncture of allowing him to vote and the responsibility that went with it, without previously subjecting him to some kind of literacy test to determine his capability of voting. South Africans were equally unaware of the rights and needs of the urban native, who had progressed far beyond the rural native mentally, and did not have sufficient provision for his physical and mental status.'[3] Half a century later, a bizarre attempt was made to denigrate her for these statements (see Chapter IX, page 165–66), though they represented 'progressive' thinking in the South African circumstances at the time.

In 1939 General Smuts, leading the United Party, had won a majority of only 13 votes in parliament to take South Africa into the war, in which, as in the

First World War, he played a major role in the War Cabinet in London. Dr DF Malan took over as a more militant leader of the overwhelmingly Afrikaner National Party. Smuts easily won the wartime 'khaki' general election in 1943 and was expected to do so again in May 1948.

Helen Suzman's submission to the Fagan Commission argued that the government must regard the African population as an integral part of South African cities. The migrant labour system should be phased out, wages increased and restrictions on enabling unskilled workers to acquire skills should be abolished. The Fagan Commission, to her disappointment, reported in favour of retaining the laws whereby all black South Africans required a pass to work in the cities, but argued that their families should be allowed to live with them and better housing should be provided. The rival Sauer Commission, set up by the National Party, came out against any liberalisation at all.

It was this issue – migrant labour – that propelled Helen Suzman into politics. She was, she said, really appalled at what she learned in the research for the evidence she was to present to the Fagan Commission. She felt that she must 'do something about these laws'.

Concluding that they could only be changed by political action, she joined the United Party in the run-up to the 1948 election.[4]

On the evening of the election, Helen Suzman was attending a performance of Sartre's play *The Flies* at Wits University when the hall emptied as the news broke that Smuts had lost his own parliamentary seat. The voting structure was still weighted heavily in favour of rural constituencies and Smuts had declined to do anything about this. As a result, he lost the election despite winning nearly 60 per cent of the votes. The National Party and its allies won the election by just five seats.

The National Party had strongly opposed South Africa's involvement in the war against Germany, with one of its future leaders, John Vorster, engaged in active subversion, and another, PW Botha, also an activist opposing the war. One of the government's first actions was to scrap the recommendation of the Fagan Commission that the permanent urbanisation of black people should be recognised in law.

As Helen Suzman said later, 'there was really no way that one could shut one's eyes'. Appalled by these developments and feeling that she must try to do something about them, she got herself appointed as the information officer of the Witwatersrand Women's Council of the United Party. Her high energy and effective oratory soon established her reputation in the party's Johannesburg branch.

As the 1953 election approached, there were high hopes that the 1948 result would turn out to have been an aberration and could be reversed. To her surprise, Helen Suzman was approached by a member of the committee of the United Party in the affluent north Johannesburg constituency of Houghton, who asked her to stand for parliament. As she said on the telephone that she couldn't, because of her job and two children, her husband asked what she was saying no to. When she explained, he said that of course she should stand: it was the natural culmination of all the work she had been doing.[5]

She won the nomination against the sitting member, who had been inactive in parliament and hardly ever visited the constituency. Once nominated for the United Party, she won the election unopposed, as the 'silk stocking' district of Houghton was a safe opposition constituency. In an election meeting at this time, she observed that: 'It is among the best educated and more civilised members of the native population that resentment is greatest.'

But the National Party increased its majority in parliament.

On being elected, she wrote to a friend: 'Even if I have the principles and try to uphold them, there is the all-powerful caucus, to keep the new girl quiet.' Still unsure whether she really wanted a full-time political career, and conscious that she was not fluent in Afrikaans, she offered to resign her seat in favour of another United Party candidate, Albert Robinson (later Sir Albert Robinson and high commissioner in Rhodesia), who, fortunately, declined. Seventy per cent of the speeches in parliament were in Afrikaans. She understood the language perfectly, but spoke it with a cut-glass English accent. Relying as she did on her eloquence and biting repartee, she made all her own parliamentary speeches in English.

She arrived in Cape Town in July 1953, 'shaking in my boots', and it did not take her long to discover that her views on race relations, based on ideas of simple justice but also on the impossibility of defying the laws of economics, were a long way to the left of most of her colleagues, convinced as they were that the only way to wrest power back from the Nationalists was to appear, especially in the rural constituencies, scarcely less conservative than they were. She described herself as 'slogging away, a little back bencher, very conscientious', learning all the time.[6]

She was given encouragement by the liberal elder statesman Harry Lawrence and especially by Harry Oppenheimer, who served as an opposition member in parliament until the death of his father, Sir Ernest Oppenheimer. She quickly became absorbed in the proceedings of the House and its committees, the detailed study of pending legislation and the attempts to amend it, the preparation of speeches and the apparently interminable meetings with her colleagues. She decided that she would make a report-back speech to her constituents at the end of every parliamentary session, a practice that reinforced the special relationship she forged with her supporters in Houghton.

Her life was not easy, as it entailed living in rented accommodation in Cape Town for six months of the year. She aimed to fly back to Johannesburg every second weekend to be with her family. Her teenage daughters were well looked after by their father and grandparents, and were happy at school in Johannesburg. A suggestion that they might go to boarding school was flatly rejected by them. They were proud of their mother and remained exceptionally close to her to the end of her life, despite living on different continents.

At a protest meeting at Wits University, Helen Suzman was asked by a black student if she would permit him to marry her daughter. Patty, who was present, suggested that the student had better ask her himself![7] Frances (Francie), who married the distinguished jurist Jeffrey (now Sir Jeffrey) Jowell, is an art historian, based in London. Patricia followed her father into the medical profession, becoming a nephrologist, based in Boston. Both were closely involved in helping to look after their mother, to the extent she would let them do so, in the last years of her life. Notwithstanding a few dramas, they were an exceptionally united family.

Moses Suzman was regarded by his colleagues in Johannesburg as no less outstanding as a physician than his wife was in the political arena. The eminent physician had an other-worldly streak. While writing in his study one evening, he was informed by a servant that there was a burglar in the yard. 'Tell the madam,' was the reply.

* * *

In parliament, Helen Suzman aligned herself with a small group of MPs who had decidedly more liberal views on race relations than the great majority of their counterparts in the United Party. The great issue at the time was the determination of the National Party to disenfranchise the limited number of members of the coloured community in the Cape who, subject to property and educational qualifications, were still qualified to vote in general elections. The measure required a two-thirds majority in both houses of parliament. One of her party colleagues, Arthur Barlow, actually supported these proposals and kept interjecting in her speeches, 'It's the lady from Lithuania again,' until told that, if he continued to do so, she would ensure that these words appeared in the parliamentary record. However, a large fraction of the party had concluded that the only way to arrest the decline in the party's electoral fortunes was to move to the right.

The United Party opposed the infamous Bantu Education Act, introduced in 1953 by Dr Verwoerd, as Minister for Native Affairs. Under 'Bantu education', black South Africans were condemned to a separate and deliberately inferior education system, to meet their supposedly limited needs. Verwoerd wanted to prevent 'the creation of frustrated people who, as a result of the education they receive, have expectations in life which the circumstances in South Africa do not allow to be fulfilled'. What, he wanted to know, was the use of teaching the Bantu child mathematics? If the 'native' was being taught to expect that he would 'live his adult life under a policy of equal rights, he is making a big mistake'.[8] Verwoerd was seeking to eliminate the influence of church schools; these, he complained, were bent on turning out 'black Englishmen', which could only lead to frustration. The Bantu, he contended, must not become a black Englishman, 'to be used against the Afrikaner'.

Helen Suzman launched attack after scathing attack on the whole concept of Bantu education. It was, she said, utterly futile to 'try and keep natives in a perpetual twilight and lead them back to a tribal Eden'.

When Helen Suzman attacked in parliament what she saw as the absurd practice of reserving entire categories of skilled jobs for white workers, she was accused by a Nationalist MP of 'trying to grind the Afrikaner worker into the dust'. She denounced the Bill prohibiting racially mixed trade unions and re-inforcing job reservation for whites even though, as she pointed out, the expansion of the South African economy meant there were not enough white workers to perform all these skilled jobs, resulting in the government having to make blanket exemptions in, for instance, the clothing industry. Why, she asked, did the government want, or need, to interfere so dramatically in the normal working of the economy – all based on the misconception that the employment of non-white workers in skilled jobs would lead to unemployment among whites? Appalled at the combined effects of job reservation and Bantu education, 30 years later, in 1985, she wrote to former World Bank president Robert McNamara that 'I really could weep when I think of all the lost years in which South Africa could have been using to the full all her human resources.'[9]

To her dismay, the United Party decided to support the Separate Amenities Bill of 1953 reserving public amenities for the white community. Despite threats from the chief whip of her party, she walked out rather than vote for the Bill. By this stage she was telling her constituents that she was 'surprised at the completely absorbing nature of the work she was doing in Parliament'.

In October the liberals in the Transvaal wing of the United Party combined to expel by a small majority a right-wing group led by Bailey Bekker who wanted to join with the government in removing coloured voters from the electoral roll. Because they refused to resign their seats, the Witwatersrand action committee, led by Max Borkum, insisted that all United Party candidates in the Transvaal henceforth sign an undertaking to resign their seats if they left the party, a pledge that was to rebound on them in due course.

In the 1954 session she denounced 'the nightmarish dreams of the Minister of Native Affairs'. She told her constituents that 'the economic integration of the Native is a fact and not a policy. And, of course, it is an ineluctable fact. More than two thirds of the Natives live outside the Native Reserves – three million of them on European farms and two million of them in the so-called European urban areas'.[10] She bitterly opposed the Natives Resettlement Bill, which was designed to eliminate 'black spots' – an obsession for Verwoerd. She did so despite what she described as monotonous interjections by her opponents, such as 'Mau Mau'. Late 1954 saw the beginning of the forced removal of the black and coloured community from Sophiatown in Johannesburg.

In May 1955 the government introduced the Senate Bill, enabling it to pack the Senate with sufficient nominees to secure the two-thirds majority of both houses of parliament, sitting together, to be able to remove the coloured voters from the common roll. When the United Party leader, JGN Strauss, began to waver on the coloured vote issue, Helen Suzman and seven other MPs threatened to resign. They were persuaded not to do so by Harry Oppenheimer, but one liberal MP, Bernard Friedman, did resign in protest at Strauss's refusal to make clear that, if elected, the United Party would restore coloured voters to the electoral roll. Friedman took the honourable course of resigning and fighting a by-election as an independent candidate in his constituency in Hillbrow, in which he was defeated.

Helen Suzman felt uneasy about not resigning with Friedman, but accepted Harry Oppenheimer's advice that she must stay and fight the issue out within the United Party caucus. In an optimistic interpretation of the party's position, she stated 'unequivocally that we will return the coloured voters when we are able to the common voters' roll'. That certainly was her position of principle, though not that of many of her colleagues. Explaining herself to her constituency committee, she said that 'while we turn our frustrations in on ourselves, the Nationalists are busy consolidating themselves ... As long as I stay in politics I shall continue to fight for my ideals.' But she wrote to a friend that she had just gone through the worst week of her life.[11]

She set off on a visit to the Congo and met Garfield Todd, the liberal prime minister of Southern Rhodesia, whose ideas about 'partnership' seemed to her to offer some promise, until he was disavowed by the white Rhodesian electorate. The chaos and civil war that accompanied Belgium's withdrawal from the Congo in 1960 were to have a major impact in hardening white attitudes and strengthening National Party support in South Africa.

During the 1956 parliamentary session, the government introduced a fresh raft of discriminatory Bills to 'preserve white civilisation in South Africa'. Helen Suzman described these as 'designed to deprive the non-Europeans of their rights by statutory means'. On 15 February, in a joint session of both houses, the government at last achieved its objective of removing coloured voters from the common electoral roll. The United Party had held fast in opposing this.

In the 1957 parliamentary session, Verwoerd introduced a Bill to further tighten controls over the influx of Africans into the urban areas. This included a provision to deter Africans from attending churches in white areas, causing an uproar even among his own supporters. Helen Suzman's criticisms were countered with anti-Semitic attacks on her, and the Bill eventually was passed. In a public speech at this time she said: 'The time is coming when the non-Europeans must be given a share in running the country. There must, however, be differentiation between the educated Native and his tribal counterpart.'[12] These ideas, however restrictive they may appear today, were light years ahead of those of her party.

At the end of 1957, the liberal group in the party was weakened when, following the death of his father, Sir Ernest Oppenheimer, Harry Oppenheimer retired from parliament to take over the chairmanship of the Anglo American Corporation. Sir De Villiers Graaff had become head of the United Party in 1956. An anglicised Afrikaner, educated at Oxford, of independent means, he had a considerable personal following both in the party and in the country. He had, Helen Suzman acknowledged, been good on the coloured vote issue, but was to prove a disappointment to the liberals in other respects. When any contentious statement was debated in party meetings, to her annoyance his favourite saying was: 'When in doubt, leave out.'

In the April 1958 election, she was unopposed in Houghton, but the United Party was severely defeated. Many of its members blamed the liberal wing of the party for the continuing decline in their electoral fortunes.

When Dr Verwoerd became prime minister in September 1958, he declared: 'I believe that the will of God was revealed in the ballot.' Helen Suzman told her constituents that South Africa was now embarked on a course of extremism with a fanatic at the helm. Verwoerd on one occasion observed that 'I never have a nagging doubt of whether I might be wrong.'[13] He sought to give an ethical basis to his vision of grand apartheid by arguing that black South Africans could enjoy full political rights, but not in white South Africa. Under the doctrine of 'separate development', blacks would exercise these rights in their own areas. The plan was to consolidate 264 separate tribal areas into eight self-governing 'Bantustans'. Verwoerd convinced not only himself but also a raft of Afrikaner intellectuals of the merits of this policy, the fatal weaknesses of which were the economic interdependence of black and white South Africans, the non-viability of the Bantustans and the denial of all rights to non-whites in the urban areas.

While Verwoerd pressed ahead with his scheme, the battle between the small liberal and larger conservative groupings within the so-called United Party was intensifying to a point at which Harry Oppenheimer wrote to Harry Lawrence that, if it came to a split, he would be on the side of the liberals, as Graaff 'seems convinced that the only thing is to accept or appear to accept the Nat view on race relations' as the only way to win back votes, especially in the rural areas.[14]

Helen Suzman by this stage was asking herself rhetorically in parliament a question that was to be used against her later: '[W]hether the opposition is not indeed rendering a disservice to the country by its presence in Parliament. I feel more and more that we are simply providing the government with a cloak of respectability.' Her answer was that they must stay and fight the government's legislation. In response to the plan for Bantu education, she asked: 'How do you teach mathematics in terms of Bantu culture? With cowrie shells?' To further annoy her opponents, she told them that the best essay she had ever read on the poor-white problem in South Africa had been written by an African student, Eduardo Mondlane. It was important, she added, that young white South Africans should realise that 'there are non-white South Africans who are their intellectual superiors'.[15]

In the run-up to the United Party conference in Bloemfontein, Graaff became reconciled to the idea that it could be for the best if Helen Suzman and two or three other left-wingers left the party. The conservative group, led by Douglas Mitchell, leader of the party in Natal, was determined to help bring this about. 'To get rid of these liberals would win us many votes,' one of them observed.

The conference took place in an atmosphere exceedingly hostile to the liberals. To her fury, Helen Suzman's speech was greeted with abuse and barracking. She was told by a colleague not to be such a 'starry-eyed idealist. You can only go as far as your electorate will let you and they won't let you go very far at all in this country'.[16]

On the following day, Mitchell put forward his motion that no more land should be handed over to black South Africans. Graaff opposed the measure, but made clear that he would not resign if it was passed. It was carried by an overwhelming majority.

Helen Suzman left the meeting determined to resign from the party. She found her close friends and colleagues Zach de Beer, Colin Eglin and Ray Swart and a handful of others equally determined to do so. Graaff was told before he left Bloemfontein of their intention to issue a statement on the land resolution, which they released that evening. This denounced the unwillingness of the party congress to face up to the 'increasingly urgent problems of our multiracial country'. They doubted, therefore, if they could 'any longer serve any honest or useful purpose as members of the party' and they intended to discuss this with Graaff. Each of them had a separate meeting with their leader. When Helen Suzman met Graaff, he made no effort to dissuade her from resigning, though he did try hard with others. He regarded her as a troublemaker and so far to the left as to be an electoral liability to the United Party.[17]

Chapter III

Bright star in a dark chamber
Chief Albert Luthuli

The rebel MPs met in Helen Suzman's house in Johannesburg on 23 and 24 August 1959 to establish the new Progressive Party, rejecting racial discrimination and proposing the vote for all adult citizens subject to educational or economic qualifications. Harry Oppenheimer, though no longer in parliament, promised them his support.

They had to decide whether to resign their seats and fight by-elections in accordance with the pledge, initiated by Max Borkum, that any of the Transvaal MPs leaving the United Party should undertake to do so. Helen Suzman wanted to resign and stand again, but the pledge did not apply to the Cape and Natal MPs and the others declined to do so. They wanted time to organise support for the new party. The minutes of the meeting concluded that they must ensure that progressive voices continued to be heard in the South African parliament while they launched the Progressive Party.

They consulted Oliver Tambo, later to become head of the ANC in exile, and travelled to see Chief Albert Luthuli, the President of the ANC, later to be awarded the Nobel Prize, who was at the time restricted to his residence in Zululand. The black leaders opposed a qualified franchise, but welcomed the birth of a new party committed to eliminating racial discrimination and abolishing the pass laws. In December, the ANC issued a statement applauding the establishment of the new party.[1] Helen Suzman did not, in this period, see anything wrong with a non-racial qualified franchise based primarily on educational qualifications as a step towards universal suffrage. The Progressive Party did not formally embrace universal suffrage until the 1970s, a move she regarded by then as long overdue.

She missed the opening of the 1960 session of

parliament due to illness. She did not, therefore, hear Harold Macmillan deliver his historic 'wind of change' speech. Macmillan later told her that he had found Verwoerd to be the most granite-like personality he had ever encountered.

In parliament, the breakaway MPs were jeered at for failing to resign their seats and fight elections under their own banner and for splitting the opposition. Helen Suzman's reply was that they had made the break 'not to split the opposition, but indeed to become the only opposition'.

On 21 March 1960 the PAC leader Robert Sobukwe called on black South Africans to protest by burning the passes they were required to obtain to work in urban areas. In the township of Sharpeville, near Johannesburg, a large crowd of unarmed blacks surrounded the police station to hand in their passes. Without any order to fire being given, a policeman lost his head and fired into the crowd, with others following suit. Sixty-nine black people were killed, many of them shot in the back as they fled the scene. Helen Suzman forced the Minister of Justice to admit, in parliament, that 186 people had been wounded. As she wrote to her daughters, 'all the evidence points to quite needless and hysterical shootings by the police'.

She had a sworn statement to that effect from a journalist who had witnessed the shootings. She told her constituents that, at this time, parliament was 'to all intents and purposes the last forum of free speech in the country'. Under parliamentary privilege she was able to ask questions and elicit information that otherwise could not or would not be reported.[2]

A state of emergency was declared. The ANC and PAC were banned, all meetings were prohibited and 1,600 people were imprisoned without trial. As the pro-government newspaper *Die Burger* observed, 'South Africa has become the polecat of the world'.

The emergency measures were not contested by the United Party. In parliament they were opposed only by Helen Suzman and her colleagues. When the government brought forward the Unlawful Organisations Bill, she argued fiercely against these measures:

> I am pleading for members to realise that banning and force and ever greater disabilities are not going to solve the difficulties in South Africa … Putting down a movement which is devoted to non-violent measures simply means that organisations which are devoted to violent measures will arise. Banning people does not mean

… that violent ideas disappear; it simply means that people go underground, that things are more difficult to control and I and you do not stop the rebellion that goes on in people's hearts against genuine grievances and genuine disabilities.[3]

It was this intervention that caused a National Party MP, Blaar Coetzee, to say: 'I forgive you; you are very naive, you are a woman.'

She also demanded, repeatedly, that the police should receive proper training and non-lethal equipment to deal with crowd control. These arguments made no impression on the government and did nothing to persuade the United Party to oppose the state of emergency or the banning of the ANC and PAC.

In response to insistent pressure from Helen Suzman, the Minister of Police made what was to turn out to be one important concession. This was that she should be allowed to visit the detainees in Pretoria jail. When she arrived, the prison officer in charge greeted her in his military uniform. As she walked in, smiles appeared on the faces of the prisoners. The commandant introduced her, but told them: 'You are not allowed to talk about any of the conditions inside the place.' A prisoner she knew, Ernie Wentzel, a member of the multiracial Liberal Party, said: 'Commandant, you mean I can't tell Mrs Suzman we're on hunger strike.'

'No, man, you can't tell her that,' the commandant replied.

'Can't I tell her we are not allowed any visitors?'

'No, you can't tell her that either.'

This continued for a while, with Helen Suzman trying hard to keep a straight face. She publicised immediately the fact that the prisoners were on hunger strike.[4]

In April, a failed assassination attempt had served only to convince Verwoerd further of his divine inspiration. On 31 May 1960, in Bloemfontein, celebrating the 50th anniversary of the Union of South Africa, Verwoerd concluded his speech by launching a dove into the air, declaring: 'There goes the symbol of South Africa's peace and prosperity.' The gesture was not a success. In Helen Suzman's words, 'the astute bird dropped like a stone.'[5]

* * *

In October 1960, Verwoerd narrowly won, by a mere 73,380 votes, a referendum proposing that South

Africa should become a republic. At the ensuing Commonwealth Prime Ministers' Conference, held in London in March 1961, his proposal that South Africa should remain a member of the Commonwealth on that basis encountered such strong resistance that he withdrew South Africa from the Commonwealth and called an early election in October 1961.

In doing so, he was able to capitalise on the fears engendered by the civil war that had erupted in the Congo. He wanted the Progressive Party to be 'wiped out in the elections because it is a dangerous party undermining the foundations of our existence in South Africa'. The 'annihilation' of the Progressives was, he said, one of the reasons why an election had become necessary.[6]

Helen Suzman had said in parliament that South Africa was fast becoming little different from an occupied country so far as the African majority were concerned. Their political organisations and trade unions were banned and their leaders banished without trial. They had absolutely no voice through the normal political channels. 'What sort of freedom is it that these people enjoy?'[7]

She was attacked by one of her constituents for having failed to resign her seat when she left the

United Party two years before. In reply she wrote that she had been elected to fight the Nationalist government. Could anyone claim that she had not fulfilled her obligations in that regard?[8]

To her constituents she read out a message of support from Chief Luthuli. The Progressive Party, she said, could not hope to take over the government. But, she inquired, did not the country have much to gain if it could show the outside world and millions of non-white South Africans that it had people prepared to oppose all forms of racial discrimination?

She had the support of the *Rand Daily Mail*, under its liberal editor Laurence Gandar, and the formidable organising skills of her campaign manager, Max Borkum, a Second World War veteran and leading stockbroker, later to become president of the Johannesburg Stock Exchange. Her supporters responded with missionary zeal. Every second tree in Houghton was plastered with her picture. Absentee voters were tracked down. At this time, it was possible to do a good deal of canvassing on foot. (In later years, in this well-heeled district, that ceased to be an option. As she put it, 'If you got past the security gates, you would be torn to pieces by the Rottweilers.' Her canvassing thereafter was done mainly by telephone, and she was able to tell by the tone in which her call was received whether the household was likely to vote for her, as most of them did.) But her ten parliamentary colleagues all were defeated. She was the only Progressive Party candidate to retain her seat. Her daughter Frances asked her, despairingly: 'What are you going to do?'

She had no idea that she would be alone in this situation for the next 13 years. She described the 1960 and 1961 parliamentary sessions as the tensest and most bitter she had experienced. She was now isolated in a chamber filled with her political opponents, who subjected her to hostile and sneering interjections every time she made a speech. Far from deterring her, these served only to increase her anger at the injustice of the laws she was opposing. As she said later of these solitary years, it was her anger that kept her going.

Prime Minister HF Verwoerd, born in the Netherlands, a doctor of psychology, was a true fanatic, convinced of his divine mission to preserve white civilisation on the southern tip of Africa. He was, she said, the only man who ever really scared her, because of the utter certainty of his convictions and the apparent coherence of his schemes, all of them based on the fundamentally false premise that there were no urbanised blacks; they all belonged in their ethnic areas. No counter-argument, however valid, could make the slightest impact on him. Verwoerd pursued with utter ruthlessness the policy of forced removals required to give effect to 'separate development'. Huge numbers of people were forcibly removed to 'resettlement areas' with no facilities to receive them, eventually creating the supposedly independent Bantustans of Transkei, Ciskei, Bophuthatswana and Venda, with no financial or any other form of genuine independence.

When Helen Suzman introduced a private member's motion to repeal those sections of the Immorality Act that made sexual relations across the colour line a criminal offence, the Minister of Justice, John Vorster, responded by attacking her for condoning immoral relations across the colour line, as if the entire coloured community did not already exist.

In 1962, opposing the repressive Sabotage Bill (later passed as the General Law Amendment Act 76 of 1962, but known as the Sabotage Act), with its incredibly broad definition of sabotage, she was so infuriated by the equivocal attitude of the United

Party that, she claimed, she saw a shiver in their ranks 'looking for a spine to run up'. Describing it as the 'Intimidation Bill' because 'the idea is to frighten the life out of anyone who disagrees with the government', she told her constituents that, 'If in order to defend South Africa against communism, it is necessary to introduce the most abhorrent features of totalitarianism into our system of government, we can no longer pretend to be a democracy.'[9]

On 18 May of that year, Chief Luthuli wrote to her to say that, together with the writer Alan Paton, he was organising a mass protest in Durban. He congratulated her on 'the gallant fight you are putting up, almost single-handed, against Nationalist tyranny'.

A question she tabled at this time revealed that, out of 11 million black South Africans, only 2,603 had a taxable income. As for the Bantustans, 'strangely enough', she declared, 'people like to enjoy rights where they live, not where they do not live'.[10]

At the beginning of 1963, six whites were murdered by members of Poqo, an extremist faction of the PAC, and there were riots by the coloured community in Paarl. Helen Suzman told parliament that, by denying them rights of political expression and economic opportunity, the government had left black

South Africans unable to express their frustration other than by violent means:

> As long as there are people who are denied rights of political expression … who live the barrack-like sort of life that the Africans live in this country, who are denied normal family life, so long will individuals and groups of individuals find some means of expressing their frustration. The Government has left such people with few measures other than violent means. It refuses to understand that if non-violent protests are not allowed, they will be replaced by violent protests. If moderate leaders are silenced, they will be replaced by extremist ones.[11]

She went on to quote Nelson Mandela's words during his trial for leaving the country illegally and organising a strike, a year before he was sentenced to life imprisonment at the Rivonia Trial:

> We have warned repeatedly that the government, by resorting continually to violence, will breed in this country counter-violence among the people, until ultimately if there is no dawning of sanity

on the part of the government the dispute between the government and my people will finish
up being settled in violence and force.[12]

In April 1963 the government presented an amended
version of the Sabotage Bill, under which people
could be detained for 90 days without charge and
then rearrested after the 90 days had expired, as the
government deemed necessary. The Bill also contained a clause enabling the government to re-detain
indefinitely a prisoner who had completed his prison
sentence, as the PAC leader Robert Sobukwe was about
to do. Sobukwe had been sentenced to three years in
prison for organising defiance of the pass laws. Vorster
described Sobukwe as a 'strong, magnetic personality,
a person who can organise' and, therefore, too dangerous to be released.[13] The provision thus became known
as the 'Sobukwe clause'.

The United Party leader, De Villiers Graaff,
criticised this vast extension of arbitrary powers. As
Helen Suzman listened to him making these critical
comments, she imagined that the United Party would
oppose the Bill. But Graaff, in conclusion, said that
his party would support the legislation because they
wanted to see law and order maintained as much as

the government did. A Nationalist newspaper gloated that 'the United Party lay down like curs'. As Helen Suzman told her constituents, 'If ever I felt sick at heart it was on the day I witnessed the tragic capitulation of the official opposition the day they supported the second reading of that monstrous Bill.'

When the parliamentary Speaker said, 'I put the question', she stood up and traced the history of non-violent opposition, which had produced no results for the black majority. 'A great number of people, who were formerly peace-loving, will be driven to desperate acts of recklessness.' There came an interjection: 'Is that a threat?' 'It is not a threat', she replied. 'I am in no position to threaten, but I am in a position to warn.' The Bill, by providing for detention without trial, which could be indefinitely extended by arbitrary decisions made by officials behind closed doors, fundamentally undermined the rule of law. 'It was the very failure of African leaders to achieve any improvement in the everyday life of the Africans that had led to the rise of extremist leaders in South Africa.'[14]

The minister thanked the official opposition for its support and said that, as usual, she was supporting the enemies of South Africa. When the Speaker again put the question, she was drowned out by all the other members of parliament shouting 'Aye'. She stood up and demanded a division, sitting on her own in a sea of empty green benches as the United Party members all voted with the government. (At this time, a single member could force a division, and she did so on a series of subsequent Bills, until the United Party combined with the government to change the rules to provide that no division could be called unless at least four members demanded it.)

Chief Luthuli wrote (see page 189) to express his 'deep appreciation and admiration for your heroic and lone stand against a most reactionary Parliament … I most heartily congratulate you for your untiring efforts in a situation that would frustrate and benumb many … For ever [sic] remember, you are a *bright Star* in [a] dark Chamber, where *lights of liberty* of what is left, are going out one by one.' He thanked her for opposing 'one of the most diabolic Bills, ever to come before Parliament. Not only ourselves – your contemporaries, but also posterity, will hold you in high esteem.'[15]

Her efforts brought a fierce reaction from her adversaries. One newspaper reported a Nationalist MP attacking her as 'a danger to us in the House … She is sweeping up hatred in this country.' She remained unflinching as she was called 'a political pest ... the biggest political enemy of the country' and attacked for her 'pestilential politics'. In the words of one parliamentary observer at the time, 'Mrs Suzman appeared to thrive on these remarks and came back time and time again with her attacks on Bantu policy.'[16]

In her report-back meeting she said:

> The task of all who believe in multiracialism in this country is to survive. Quite inevitably, time is on our side ... I am absolutely certain that ... sooner or later a settlement will have to be reached between moderate whites and moderate non-whites. Apart from external and internal pressures, economics alone will compel this. The immediate present belongs to the extremists, but the future belongs to us.[17]

She opened the 1964 parliamentary session by citing innumerable statements by non-white detainees, all alleging different forms of torture, including the use of electric shocks. The Commissioner of Police's denials of all these allegations were simply incredible, she said. She reported to her constituents that 'apartheid and the rule of law are mutually incompatible'.

She campaigned fiercely against a Bill reinforcing the pass laws, which continued to criminalise black people and their families looking to work in the urban areas. The result was that 1,000 people a day were going to jail in South Africa for infringing the pass laws. 'The only conclusion one can reach', she said, 'is that the government does not consider the black man as a human being ... It ignores all the fundamental concepts of human dignity ... It reduces him to the level of a chattel.'[18] Half the population, she said bitterly in parliament, seemed to be occupied in handing out permits to the other half.

She remained completely undeterred by the personal attacks now made regularly on her in parliament. 'I can't say I'm blameless,' she observed, 'since I'm provocative. Most of the questions I put were embarrassing.' Told that her days in parliament were numbered, she asked her opponents how they intended to achieve this: 'Are you going to put me under house arrest or send me to Robben Island?'

However, in March 1964 an article in *Die Burger* commented that 'she is putting up a parliamentary performance which is impressing even her enemies.

For one person alone to state her party's viewpoint on every item of legislation is crippling work … and she is doing it well.' The National Party MP for Rustenburg said: 'In her fight for the Bantu, the honourable member sings the same tune for year after year. One must admire her for the fight she is putting up.' Verwoerd himself, while detesting her ideas and the causes she espoused, was obliged to acknowledge that she was an 'outstanding parliamentarian with well-considered arguments'.[19]

She told the government that 'there will always be unrest in South Africa unless the basic injustices are set right': it was no use adopting the ostrich-like attitude of pretending that it was all the work of communists and agitators. Citing the 750th anniversary of the Magna Carta, which enshrined the principle of *habeas corpus*, she declared that in South Africa the last vestiges of this fundamental right were being destroyed.

The banned anti-apartheid activist Helen Joseph wrote to her in 1965 to wish her 'Good luck for the session and your gallant lonely fight. I sometimes think that I am far less lonely in house arrest than you in a hostile House.' During that session, in a private member's motion, she moved that any statute that deprived citizens of their liberty without recourse to the courts should be repealed. As the members of the United Party sat in stony silence, she rounded on them, saying, 'Why do you not get up? Are you not going to support the rule of law?' She told her constituents that she had been voted into parliament 'to represent a point of view that exists in South Africa – despite intimidation, despite the unfavourable climate, despite the bullying of the government and the toadying of the one-time anti-government forces … If mine is the voice of dissent it is so because conditions in South Africa call out for such a voice.'[20]

When, in 1966, Verwoerd showed support for Ian Smith's unilateral declaration of independence (UDI) in Rhodesia, Helen Suzman argued that South Africa should have nothing to do with the Smith regime. She denounced the strategy of the United Party, which was to show even more ardent support for Smith and his colleagues than the government was doing: 'The whole United Party Congress at Bloemfontein was on its feet, led by its leader, giving three cheers for Mr Smith.' Siding with Smith, she said, would simply lead to South Africa's being ostracised alongside the Rhodesians. Verwoerd's response was to say that he had written her off, to which she replied: 'And the whole world has written you off.'[21]

By this time she had made such an impact in parliament that the *Sunday Times*, which supported her opponents in the United Party, published a leading article entitled 'A Special Case': 'Mrs Suzman, after all, has carved a special place for herself in South African public life. Adherents of every party admire her for her courageous and intelligent showing in Parliament ... no other candidate, not even the Prime Minister himself, has a better claim to go back.' The black newspaper the *Post* wrote: 'It is not our job to tell the whites whom to vote for. We make an exception in the case of Helen Suzman ... this doughty fighter, this most respected opponent of the government. The good wishes of millions of our people are with you.' The *World* hailed her solitary victory in Houghton as 'the news of the year for Africans. Many township people sat next to their radios waiting for the results'. The *Post* saluted her victory as a 'glorious exception'. The *New York Times* wrote that 'she actually represents more South Africans than all the other members of Parliament combined'.[22]

The Nationalists, however, had won two thirds of the seats in parliament, and had won the support of many English-speaking South Africans, especially in Natal, who hitherto had supported the United Party.

She told her constituents that now she 'was not only faced with Nats and flanked by Nats, but I have them sitting behind me, too'. Turning round, she found herself confronted 'with several sets of beady eyes fixed on me with unblinking hostility', not to mention all the uncomplimentary interjections she could hear when she made a speech.[23]

At 2.15 pm on 6 September 1966 the bells were ringing for the start of a parliamentary debate. On her front-bench seat, Helen Suzman was reading a letter when there was a strangled cry and a huge commotion across the aisle from her. Verwoerd had been stabbed fatally by a parliamentary messenger, Dimitri Tsafendas. Down the aisle rushed the Minister of Defence, PW Botha, 'arms flailing and eyes bulging'. He stopped in front of Helen Suzman, shouting to his colleagues in Afrikaans: 'Now it's war; it's these liberalists, we will get them all.' He repeated: 'The liberalists and the communists – now it's war.' Turning to her and brandishing his finger in her face, he said to her: 'It's you, you and the liberalists – you are responsible for this – you are inciting them – you.' She told Botha: 'Control yourself; stop being so hysterical. What nonsense are you talking? What have I got to do with this? You must be mad.'

She was, she said, beside herself with rage and amazement at this accusation and the threat implicit in what he had said. She reported the attack on her verbatim to the secretary of parliament. Next morning she was summoned to see the Speaker, HJ Klopper, and found PW Botha there as well. Botha glared at her and muttered: 'In terms of the rules of the House, I apologise.' Helen Suzman exploded, saying to the Speaker: 'Do you expect me to accept an apology like that?' She told Botha: 'How dare you talk to me the way you did?' What did she expect, he replied, 'There was my leader dying at my feet.' 'I'll tell you what I expect. I expect you to control yourself,' she replied. 'You're the man behind the guns in South Africa. You're the Minister of Defence. It would be a sad day for all of us if you can't control yourself'.

The Speaker begged her to accept the apology, however unsatisfactory. There were to be plenty of other instances of PW Botha's inability to control himself. From this day on, she refused to have any dealings with Botha, save for her relentless attacks on him across the floor in parliament. It took more than 20 years for her to agree to any meeting with him, until in 1988 she did so to argue for the lives of the Sharpeville Six.[24]

Chapter IV

*He should go into the townships, heavily
disguised as a human being*

Helen Suzman to Prime Minister John Vorster

As the sole member of parliament from 1961 to 1974 to argue for a non-racial future for South Africa, Helen Suzman became a sort of national ombudsman on behalf of the voiceless and the dispossessed. The Helen Suzman archive in the William Cullen Library at Wits University is a testimony to the huge volume of correspondence she received from and on behalf of prisoners and detainees and the victims of forced removals, police brutality and the multiple injustices of the regime. She dealt with all of this correspondence meticulously, leaving the reader wondering how on earth she managed this. Her daughters described her as a Basuto pony, an animal renowned for its stamina and endurance. She needed those qualities and more as she sought relentlessly to pursue the worst cases of abuse directly with the ministers and officials involved, making innumerable interventions in parliament as well as site visits to see for herself what was happening and who was responsible for it.

The archive is a demonstration of the extraordinary lengths to which she went over four decades, often in the most unpromising circumstances, to show her support for, and to secure practical improvements in, the lives of those affected by the arbitrary actions of the regime. The list of those on whose behalf she interceded reads like a who's who of the liberation struggle. As she many times told the government, what infuriated her most was the refusal of virtually every other member of parliament ever to go to see for themselves the impact on ordinary human beings of the laws they passed.

Verwoerd was succeeded as prime minister by John Vorster. During the Second World War, Vorster had been detained for two years on suspicion of treason for his attempts to disrupt the Allied war effort. Although, like PW Botha, he claimed thereafter to have been anti-war rather than pro-German, Helen Suzman noted his adherence at the time to the underground Ossewabrandwag, which she regarded as a pro-Nazi Afrikaner organisation whose declared aim was to found a one-party authoritarian state.[1]

As she wrote to US Senator Robert Kennedy on 28 October 1966, Vorster was far less awe-inspiring than Verwoerd, more earthbound, with much less of a divine mission about him. But he was no less committed to the indefinite preservation of white domination and determined to use all the resources of the state to ensure it. In personal terms she noted what 'a very formidable, unsmiling, hostile person he was to me.'[2]

Helen Suzman enjoyed telling the story of the press photographer who urged the grim-faced prime minister to smile. 'But I am smiling,' Vorster replied, though, as the photographer confirmed to her, he was unable to detect any sign of this. (Years later, when Nelson Mandela attended the wedding reception of his daughter Zindzi, he refused to say a word to Winnie Mandela, with whom he had just fallen out. His expression was so grim that Helen Suzman told him to stop trying to look like John Vorster, eliciting a wintry smile from him!)

On becoming prime minister, Vorster retained the Police and Prisons portfolio, signifying where his priorities lay. Helen Suzman regarded him as happiest, politically speaking, with a truncheon in his hand. Leaving parliament one day, she found some Ratel armoured cars drawn up outside. Looking through one of the ports of the leading Ratel, she was alarmed to find the prime minister glaring at her balefully from inside the vehicle.[3]

She sought many meetings with Vorster on behalf of detainees, in which he accorded her a correct but generally chilly reception. After one such meeting, she wrote to a friend that Vorster had declined to reveal the number of those detained. 'He was far too affable for my liking – very much like the cat that had swallowed the canary.'[4] He paid her the compliment of saying that she was worth ten United Party MPs, but contended that she allowed herself to be used. This was an allegation she accepted to be true, as she constantly intervened on behalf of people of radically different views, including all the leaders of the SACP and many extreme black nationalists. She continued to wage in parliament a relentless campaign against detentions without trial and the 'refined torture of solitary confinement'. She provided chapter and verse for her many accusations of torture, including the use of electric shocks. She could not afford to provide the names of prisoners, who would be subject to reprisals, but repeatedly told Vorster in parliament that he had no credibility whatever in denying these allegations.

The journalist Ruth First, a convinced communist and wife of Joe Slovo (later to become head of the SACP), was detained and then re-detained in 1963. There were fears on the part of her friends that she might commit suicide (as in fact she attempted to do). First's mother initially asked Helen Suzman not to intervene, but then there came a telephone call from Bram Fischer, a prominent lawyer and the clandestine leader of the Communist Party. 'Is that my favourite MP?' he inquired. 'Come off it, Bram. You don't have much choice,' was her reply. She did raise Ruth First's case with Vorster, persuading him to grant an exit visa.

Ruth First wrote to congratulate her on her 'sledge-hammer attack' on the 90-day Detention Bill (later passed as the General Law Amendment Act 37 of 1963), which made provision for detention for up to 90 days without access to counsel, adding that the anti-Nationalist fight had been 'whittled down to the efforts of one intrepid member'. She asked for help in securing an exit visa for her mother, which Helen Suzman succeeded in obtaining for her. Ruth First subsequently was killed in exile by a letter bomb sent to her by agents of the South African security police.[5]

One of Helen Suzman's guiding rules as a parliamentarian, and one of the principal reasons for her effectiveness, was always to go and see for herself what she was intervening about. This took her to the sites of many of the forced removals and the totally inadequate 'resettlement areas'. She reported in parliament, in a speech a government MP described as being full of 'hatred and malice', that thousands of people had been left on the veld, sometimes in midwinter, with tents they did not even know how to erect, no medical facilities, no schooling and no way of obtaining supplies or finding employment. Apart from these massive displacements of the black population, she forced an admission that half a million coloured and Indian families had been removed as well.

In 1967, opposing further repressive legislation under the Terrorism Act, she was accused by the Minister of Justice of always interceding 'for elements that seek to bring about the downfall of the white man in this country'. Another government MP said he was tired of her 'constant nagging about the rule of law'. The Act was described by the pro-government paper *Beeld* as 'giving the police a free hand to act without legal restraint'.[6]

She found herself constantly asked to intervene in cases of persons whose lives were damaged by their racial classification under the Population Registration Act, bedrock of all the apartheid laws. The Act caused immense hardship to those who sought to marry or cohabit as a family across the colour lines. Many hundreds of people tried to get themselves reclassified from coloured to white, with many seeking her help in their efforts to do so. She again attempted to introduce a Bill that would repeal the provisions of the Immorality Act prohibiting sex across the colour line, under which 11,000 people had been convicted. To her delight, an utter nonsense was made of all these laws in 1968 when, in South Africa's second heart transplant operation, a coloured heart was implanted in a Jewish patient.

She constantly warned the government that, far from contributing to the country's security, the laws they were passing in defiance of the interests and wishes of 70 per cent of the population were storing up immense resentment, resistance and trouble for the future. In June 1968 she told Vorster that he appeared sincerely to believe in the concept of separate development. 'How he manages to persuade himself of this in the teeth of all the evidence to the contrary is beyond me.' The real motivation was to maintain the status quo – white domination. The number of arrests under the pass laws had reached half a million a year. The government could not go on treating people like aliens in the land of their birth, denying them the most elementary human rights, including the right to live with their families. 'They will not be able to go on like this. They should realise that they are endangering the security of South Africa in their arrogance, believing that they can go on without let or hindrance in this utterly irresponsible and heartless fashion.'[7]

In 1969 she introduced a private member's motion to abolish the death penalty, a cause about which she felt passionately. This had no chance of success at the time, with the entire opposition as well as the government voting against abolition, but, many years later, she took particular satisfaction from its abolition under the constitution of post-apartheid South Africa. She also campaigned for reform of the country's anti-drugs legislation, which criminalised marijuana use with a mandatory minimum two-year prison sentence. The result was 80,000 convictions over five years for the possession of dagga (marijuana), in widespread use particularly among the non-white population. These activities led her and her party to be stigmatised by the government as soft on drugs and law and order, which did not deflect her from pursuing these causes.[8]

She described herself at this time as 'a small, fierce if somewhat inadequate watchdog for civil rights' and the interests of the disenfranchised.[9] In parliament, she had pleaded for clemency for Bram Fischer when the Communist Party leader was sentenced to life imprisonment in 1966. She also took up the cause of South Africa's most distinguished playwright, Athol Fugard, who was denied a passport for several years.

Through these 13 solo years in parliament, she felt at times very lonely. She had no colleagues to sit with in the dining room, where members sat with their party colleagues, and none to share a postmortem drink with at the end of the parliamentary day. She had no large team of people to help her, and every one of her speeches was written solely by her. She depended on her secretary, Barbara Mouat, and her one indispensable researcher, Jacqueline Beck. Yet, despite these slender resources, her research was always meticulous.

It was a source of great pride to her that, in all the debates in which she participated, she was never tripped up on a point of fact. She tabled around 200 questions every year, nearly all of them about the treatment of non-white South Africans. When an infuriated government minister shouted at her in parliament that 'You put these questions just to embarrass South Africa overseas', she replied: 'It is not my questions that embarrass South Africa: it is your answers!'[10]

In posing all these questions and pursuing all the issues she did, she was able to rely on an increasingly extensive network of correspondents who constantly appealed to her to expose the abuses they witnessed. She was in close contact with, and sought to protect, the Defence and Aid Fund, which was constantly being threatened by the government, and the Legal Resources Centre, established in 1979 and headed by Arthur Chaskalson, later to become Chief Justice of the Constitutional Court under the 1996 constitution. She tried in vain to protect the Christian Institute headed by Dr Beyers Naudé. But a host of distinguished lawyers, led by Jules Browde, George Bizos, John Dugard and Geoff Budlender, were available to offer her advice on legal issues and were in constant touch with her about cases that concerned them.

She had won the grudging respect of some of her opponents in parliament, helped by her undoubted sex appeal. Some of them regarded her with appalled fascination. One used to send her a chocolate in an envelope from time to time across the floor of the House. According to her, she achieved a boost in popularity as a result of the Israel's success in the 1967 Six-Day War. 'Good shooting, Helen!' was the response she got from a number of National Party MPs.[11]

The astonishing amount of mail she received asking for help came, nearly all of it, from the disenfranchised. No letter went unanswered. Nor did she ever fail to pursue with the authorities any of the innumerable cases in which she felt an injustice had been done.

However hard the going and however dark the circumstances around her, she never ever lost her coruscating sense of humour. When the head of an ultra-conservative Afrikaner women's group wrote to tell her that her ancestors had taken the Bible across the mountains to the savages on the other side, and made the mistake of inquiring what her ancestors were doing at the time, Helen Suzman replied that her ancestors had been busy writing the Bible.

She was on the itinerary of every visiting journalist

or dignitary, which made her feel, she said, like a surrogate Kruger National Park. When Senator Robert Kennedy visited South Africa in 1966, she described the visit as 'something of a circus', but was most grateful for the support he gave to the liberal English-speaking universities under siege, boosting the morale of 'all of us under attack' and writing to her of the inspiration he and others should draw from 'knowing that Helen Suzman never gave up'.[12]

She was fortunate to have HJ Klopper, a hard-line Nationalist and the first chairman of the secret Afrikaner Broederbond, as Speaker of the House. He ended up in the far-right Conservative Party. He told her that he did not agree with a word she said; nevertheless, it was his duty to ensure that she had every opportunity to say it. In fact, he allowed her more speaking time than any ten other MPs combined. When, on one occasion, she was ordered out of the House for failing to hear a ban by him on further interjections, a Nationalist MP who shouted 'Good riddance!' was immediately expelled as well.

The journalist Donald Woods, in the parliamentary gallery at the time, noted that the hard-boiled ultra-conservative Speaker had developed a decided weakness for the good-looking member for

Houghton, who never failed to catch his eye when she wished to speak.[13]

* * *

Although the government had won a massive majority in the 1966 election, they were alarmed at the success of two coloured candidates allied to the Progressive Party in the Cape provincial council elections. They feared that in the next election the Progressive Party would win the four seats still reserved in Parliament for coloured representatives elected by their own community. Their response was to bring forward the Prohibition of Improper Interference Bill, intended to prevent opposition parties winning non-white votes, by abolishing multiracial political parties.

Helen Suzman pictured 'some cynical official ... cackling to himself' as he came up with 'this extraordinary Bill' with the simple objective of preventing the Progressives from winning the four coloured seats.[14] It took the government two years to get the Bill through parliament, but they succeeded in May 1968. The result was the extinction of the multiracial Liberal Party, committed to universal suffrage, led by Alan Paton.

In Helen Suzman's report to her constituents, she

said that she and her colleagues had no doubt that they were right to continue as a party. That was what their non-white supporters wanted them to do; 'It is very definitely what the government does not want us to do.'[15]

Alan Paton threw his support wholeheartedly behind her. A few years later he wrote to her that 'All of us ... began to look more and more to you' as the champion of all they believed in. 'How you continue to do it, day after day, in that hostile or, at best, indifferent house, in the face of continuous and contemptuous interruption, we do not quite understand.' The word he thought it most appropriate to use in describing her was 'tough'. That, he said, left out a host of other qualities.[16]

In the same session, she protested at the ninth year of Robert Sobukwe's detention for a three-year prison sentence. As for the debate within Afrikanerdom between *verkramptes* (reactionaries) and *verligtes* (more enlightened), she had, she said, yet to find any *verligtes* on the National Party benches.

In 1969, when the MCC did not at first select a coloured cricketer, Basil D'Oliveira, to play for England against South Africa, the Nationalist Minister of Police announced this triumphantly at a party meeting. When D'Oliveira subsequently was included in the team, the prime minister, Vorster, refused to allow it to tour South Africa, a decision denounced by Helen Suzman as completely self-defeating. 'The chances are that we will find ourselves excluded from more and more international sporting events, as a result of the government's absurd and rigid attitude.' To the dismay of the sports-loving member for Houghton, the incident triggered the progressive exclusion of South Africa from international sport. The government had, she said, to change fundamentally its attitude to multiracial sport: 'Otherwise we are out of sport internationally.'[17]

When a newspaper survey suggested that over 70 per cent of the white population thought that Vorster was doing a good job and only 0.3 per cent that he was no good, she told him in parliament that she wanted to stand up and be counted among the 0.3 per cent.[18]

At the end of the year, the Nationalist newspaper *Die Vaderland* wrote of the tenth anniversary of the Progressive Party: 'It was actually a matter of congratulating one woman, Helen Suzman, without whose capability and acute bellicosity the Party would have long withered in the political wilderness.'[19]

In the April 1970 election, Helen Suzman increased her majority despite a United Party pamphlet against her, entitled 'Are these the deeds of a South African?', which attacked her for a supposed lack of patriotism and support of terrorism. Distressed at the narrow defeat of Colin Eglin in the Sea Point constituency in Cape Town, she reflected on the prospect of 'five more years alone with that bloody mob!' As this was reported in *Life* magazine, the Speaker made her apologise.

In each election, she had steadily increased her majority in Houghton. In this she was aided by an army of volunteers passionately committed to her, and by the efforts of Max Borkum. He used to disconcert her by closing his eyes and appearing to sleep soundly through her impassioned report-back speeches, only reopening them amid the torrent of applause at the end. He more than made up for this by his outstanding organising and fundraising abilities and by an enduring close friendship with her.

Her friend and cousin, Irene Menell, became chairman of her constituency party and later was elected to the Transvaal provincial council. Another great friend and ally was Selma Browde, a distinguished physician, who was elected to the Johannesburg City Council. Among the next generation, she had a particularly high regard for Ann Bernstein, future director of the Centre for Development and Enterprise, and Rhoda Kadalie, academic and activist, as the kind of fiercely independent commentators she admired. Her memoirs include a heartfelt tribute to Max Borkum, 'without whom my career would have ended in 1961'.[20]

Throughout her political career Helen Suzman enjoyed the support of a determined army of South African women who thought like her. The Black Sash organisation was formed in 1955 by a group of women who wore black sashes to mourn the violation of the constitution by the Nationalists, at the time when they were determined to expel coloured voters from the common electoral roll. The Black Sash remained an effective lobbying and support organisation for the families of prisoners and detainees, and stayed in constant contact with Helen Suzman regarding the plight of those they were trying to help.

* * *

In December 1970 Helen Suzman travelled to Zambia to meet President Kenneth Kaunda. She found him engaged in economic 'reforms' that amounted to nationalisation, and wondered how on earth he hoped to attract investment in the future. But they got on well in personal terms. She found him an engaging personality, 'full of smiling charm' and uncompromising about the Smith regime in Rhodesia.[21]

She did not meet Oliver Tambo, head of the ANC, who was based in Lusaka at this time. Any such meeting would have been ruthlessly exploited by the National Party. The result was a bitter article in the ANC journal *Sechaba* in March 1971, in which the following appeared above Tambo's name:

> Vorster, Suzman and lesser agents of colonialism have turned Africa into a veritable hunting ground for stooges and indigenous agents of racism. Mrs Suzman deserves special mention: This sweet bird from the blood-stained south flew into Zambia and sang a singularly sweet song:
>
> I am opposed to apartheid;
> I am opposed to the isolation of South Africa;
> I am opposed to violence;
> I am opposed to guerrillas ...
> I know the Africans can do nothing to cause political change in South Africa;

> I am in favour of change;
>
> Clearly in favour of change, but determined to prevent change.

Whether this was in fact written by Tambo himself remains unclear, especially in view of his later tributes to her. Many of his statements were drafted for him, and the SACP, solidly entrenched in the ANC secretariat, was bitterly hostile to Helen Suzman, whom they saw as a rival in garnering support from black South Africans, notwithstanding her numerous interventions on behalf of SACP prisoners in jail. The blank verse style is reminiscent of the literary pretensions of another prominent member of the ANC secretariat at the time.

* * *

In the 1971 parliamentary session, she launched a general attack on the government in characteristically prophetic terms. They were continuing to reserve most skilled jobs for whites, who were incapable of filling all such jobs. The Bantustans devised by the 'lofty intellect' of Verwoerd were economically unviable. There were more black South Africans – eight million of them – living in 'white' South Africa than in the so-called homelands. Her mind boggled at the thought of the grotesque society the South African government deliberately was creating for the African people.

Attacking once again the savage minimum sentences imposed mainly on black South Africans for the use of dagga, she was accused by the United Party spokesman for justice as 'having nothing but a lot of principles she waffles about'.[22]

She could be intransigent even with some of her natural supporters. Her campaign to decriminalise the use of dagga was unpopular with her party colleagues, who feared that it could cost them votes. Years later, however, she succeeded in this campaign, as minimum mandatory sentences were abandoned in cases of this kind.

For an entire parliamentary session, she boycotted the liberal editor of the *Sunday Times*, Joel Mervis, and his even more distinguished political correspondent, Stanley Uys, one of her greatest allies, because of the paper's continued support for the United Party (a decision of the board, not the editor).

To her amazement, Vorster told the *Sunday Telegraph* correspondent that he was 'not aware that there were any annoying elements in apartheid'.[23] She went through all the annoying elements he might experience if he were not white, later suggesting that he should go into the townships 'heavily disguised as a human being' to find out for himself what life was like for black South Africans.

She wrote at the time to a friend that the long stretch of sandy beach at Muizenberg, where she went swimming when in Cape Town, was 'peppered with disgusting signs saying "Reserved for Whites Only" and the non-whites … have to go for miles and miles to find a portion of beach and sea so kindly set aside for them by their white masters! It all makes me quite sick.'[24] After one of these blistering attacks on the government, a supporter wrote to say that, if she had been an early Christian, he would have had to feel sorry for the lions.

Later that year, she visited a number of other African countries with Colin Eglin. They were given a rousing cheer in the Kenyan parliament and a warm reception in Tanzania by President Julius Nyerere, who told her: 'Mrs Suzman, when all this is over, the role that you played will be remembered.'[25] On her return, she observed that they had got a good reception elsewhere in Africa 'not because of Mr Eglin's beauty or my brains', but because they represented enlightened South Africans.

Back in South Africa, the censorship board afforded a favourite target, having incurred her ire for banning over 700 books a year, including *I, Claudius* by Robert Graves and works by Émile Zola. She was delighted when an outraged filmmaker denounced the film censors as 'those old tannies' (aunts) since, as she pointed out, two of them had only school certificates, while the third did have a degree – in music.[26]

In her report-back meeting, she said that she seemed to have become the honorary ombudsman for all those who had no vote and no MP. 'I get dozens of pathetic letters smuggled out of jail and many appeals for help from banned people. Sometimes I manage to get conditions alleviated – often not. But my desk here and in Cape Town is a sad harvest of the seeds of apartheid.'[27] She was being subjected to rudeness and hostility from the prime minister and others, to which she was inured. 'After all, I like them as little as they like me.'

She had an ugly scene with PW Botha, 'hardly a model of self-control', during the Defence vote over Jehovah's Witnesses being subjected to solitary confinement as conscientious objectors and then being rearrested as soon as their sentences ended. This had resulted in one Witness being rearrested for six consecutive periods of solitary confinement. In response, PW Botha 'went off like a Roman candle'. He roared at her 'with his customary charm – I was the mouthpiece for all who broke the law, I wanted chaos in South Africa.'[28] Yet she won the argument: in future, Jehovah's Witnesses were no longer rearrested once they had served their sentences.

In another debate, PW Botha denounced her as being the official mouthpiece of permissiveness and all subversive activities in South Africa, a remark the Speaker made him withdraw. *Die Burger* asked: 'Why has it become necessary in recent times to attack Mrs Suzman so sharply? Surely it cannot be because she gets under the skin of the Nationalists?'[29] In the course of the session she suggested ironically that the government might consider declaring Soweto also a 'homeland', as Johannesburg was nowhere near any of the homelands. Verwoerd's idea that millions of black people would start streaming back to the Bantustans had proved to be absurd.

During the parliamentary session, she had been obliged to rush to St George's Cathedral in Cape Town to prevent demonstrating students from being beaten up by uniformed and plain-clothes police wielding batons. To her astonishment, the Minister of Police claimed that the police had acted with great tolerance and that the protests were the result of a foreign conspiracy. The prime minister said that he would have been disappointed in the police if they had not acted as they did.

During the 1973 parliamentary session, the government announced its intention to impose five-year restriction orders on eight white students it accused of subversion. Helen Suzman doubted that any of the students would be found guilty of any crime in a court of law and pronounced herself aghast at the United Party's acquiescence in these measures. The government thereupon banned eight black students, 'no doubt to show its lack of racial bias' she sarcastically observed, including the teenage Dikgang Moseneke, the future Deputy Chief Justice of the Constitutional Court. Her response was that 'the government can ban leaders and others will rise in their place because the government has itself spawned an indestructible black nationalism'.[30]

In a clash with one of her favourite targets, the Deputy Minister of Police, Jimmy Kruger, she exposed the fact that, in the first two months of the year, the police had shot 92 people attempting to escape custody. Instead of expressing regret for this, Kruger turned on her 'like a maddened snake', accusing her of treachery.[31] In another intervention, she demanded full trade union rights for black South African workers. As one commentator observed: 'It takes guts to stand up there alone to tackle not only a tough and ruthless government, but a bitter and resentful opposition.'

Helen Zille, now leader of the Democratic Alliance (DA), recalls a visit to parliament to hear Helen Suzman speak at this time. She saw her on the green benches of the old parliamentary chamber, surrounded by 'a sea of political adversaries, mostly granite-faced, dark-suited men. It was intimidating enough from the gallery. When she rose to speak there was some heckling, but also a tangible respect from the House, not only for parliament and its procedures, but for the intellect and integrity of a world-class adversary.'[32]

The interjections to which she continuously was subject are revealing of the enormous distance between her and her opponents in parliament. Suzman's responses were never temporising, but were uncompromising. When, in the early years of her parliamentary career, an incredulous National Party member asked if she really was advocating the same pay for blacks and whites, he was told that was exactly what she was demanding. Asked if she was in favour of demonstrations, she said that of course she was in favour of demonstrations: 'What a silly question.' Demonstrations were part of any normally functioning democracy.[33]

In June 1973, in the Sheldonian Theatre at Oxford, the degree of Honorary Doctor of Civil Law was conferred on her by former prime minister Harold Macmillan, to thunderous applause.

The Progressive Party organised a dinner in Cape Town to mark her 21 years in parliament. The toast was proposed by Mangosuthu Buthelezi, Chief Minister of KwaZulu, who had refused 'independence' for his homeland. He declared that she had earned 'the intense love of admirers and the intense hatred of her enemies'. She had succeeded in inspiring people from all sections of a very heterogeneous society. 'She symbolises the one flickering flame of liberty amidst the darkness that is such an enveloping feature of South African politics.' She had earned herself a niche not just in the history of South Africa, but 'one in the whole history of man's struggle for liberty'. To her amusement, Buthelezi added that she had 'a man's brain'. He knew, he said, that she would find this compliment offensive if it came from anyone other than a traditional Zulu chief! He ended by describing her as the lone voice of millions of voiceless people.[34]

She found, during these lonely years, that her most helpful allies were the press. Joseph Lelyveld published a long article about her ('Minority of One') in the *New York Times Magazine* on 20 March 1966. She also had support from many of the diplomats serving in South Africa at this time, in particular the British ambassador, Sir John Maud, and the US ambassador, Bill Edmondson.

Chapter V

Our Lady of the Prisoners
Breyten Breytenbach

As she was unable to prevent the government from locking up many of its political opponents, Helen Suzman devoted part of her formidable energies to looking after the interests of the prisoners and working doggedly to secure their release. This is how her efforts looked to someone on the other side of the prison walls – Breyten Breytenbach, the Afrikaner writer, poet and prisoner himself:

I don't think it would be excessive to say that the prisoners, both political and common-law, regard her as Our Lady of the Prisoners. She is indeed a living myth among the people inhabiting the world of shadows. The quality of the food suddenly improves? Out of the blue a movie is shown on a Saturday afternoon? People have been sleeping for years on mats on the floor ... and now beds are made available? Prisoners would look at one another and nod their heads wisely and say, 'You see, Aunty Helen did it after all'.

At the same time she was or is considered the final recourse for any prisoner, the ultimate threat of retribution or redress one would brandish when trying to get something done ...

They, the *boere*, to put it mildly, didn't like her overmuch. They detested her sharp eye and her sharp tongue and her fearless criticism of whatever wrongs she saw.

The only time I actually saw her was from the back as she walked briskly over an empty courtyard behind the workshops. The stores I worked in then gave onto the same courtyard. She was surrounded by a cohort of nervous and angry prison officials, grinding their teeth in impotent rage and hoping to shoo her off as rapidly as possible.[1]

From 1960, Helen Suzman succeeded in her campaign to be allowed to visit prisoners, as she investigated the conditions of the detainees under the state of emergency. Nelson Mandela recalled having a consultation in 1963 in Pretoria Central prison with his lawyer, Bram Fischer, while they were preparing for the Rivonia Trial. Fischer 'whispered almost in reverence as a woman passed in the corridor: "Helen Suzman."' Mandela found this 'significant coming from a man whose political views would not normally lead him to respect a liberal'.[2]

In 1965 the *Rand Daily Mail* was prosecuted for publishing articles about prison conditions. She insisted on being allowed to revisit Pretoria Central to examine the conditions there. When she arrived, it was clear that there had been an overnight transformation, with the prisoners wearing new clothes and hot water suddenly available.

She had managed to get permission to visit the political prisoners in Pretoria Central once a year. She was particularly concerned about Bram Fischer, Rhodes scholar, lawyer and leader of the SACP, who remained a convinced communist even after the Soviet repression in Hungary in 1956 and Czechoslovakia in 1968. On one occasion when she visited him, he presented her with a bunch of flowers from the prison yard.

Finding him desperately ill with cancer, she told the press that, when so many millions were being spent on security, she had no idea why the government remained afraid of one bedridden and incapacitated man. In early March 1975, she visited Fischer again and found him gaunt and frail. She told Kruger (by then Minister of Justice) that Fischer was dying, and, when Kruger said that he could not release him, she insisted that he should be released into the care of his brother. Kruger subsequently claimed that Fischer was recovering, and wanted to rearrest him, but was told by Helen Suzman: 'You will do no such thing.' Kruger gave way and Fischer remained until his death in the care of his family. The Helen Suzman papers contain a heartfelt tribute from Bram Fischer's daughters for all the efforts she made on his behalf.[3]

She intervened repeatedly on behalf of activist Barbara Hogan, later to be a cabinet minister in the South African government, when she was convicted of treason and given a savage ten-year sentence for passing information to the ANC about trade union activities.[4]

She continued to receive hundreds of letters smuggled out of jail from prisoners. The usual reaction of the Commissioner for Prisons, with whom she raised all these cases, was to claim that the complaints had been investigated and found to have no substance. But she was assured by the prisoners themselves that the fact that the prison authorities knew that she was seeking to hold them accountable did have an effect on their behaviour.

* * *

In February 1967 she managed at last to get permission to visit Robben Island, 11km off the coast of Cape Town. The strong currents, chilly water and sharks in Table Bay rendered escape effectively impossible. She was appalled at the conditions she found on the island. Among the life prisoners were Nelson Mandela, Walter Sisulu and much of the rest of the leadership of the ANC. She introduced herself to one prisoner, Eddie Daniels, who said that they knew all about her. He directed her straight to Mandela in his cell as, he declared, 'our leader'. Mandela stuck his hand through the bars to greet her. 'It was,' he said, 'an odd and wonderful sight to see this courageous woman peering into our cells and strolling around our courtyard.'

She was struck from the outset by his extraordinary self-assurance and commanding presence, vis-à-vis both his fellow prisoners and the prison officers. He complained about a particular warder, one Van Rensburg, who had a swastika tattooed on the back of his hand. They were all doing hard labour in the quarry and Van Rensburg was determined to make life as difficult as possible for them. The prisoners were allowed few visits, were sleeping on bedrolls on the floor of their cells, the food was bad and they were not allowed newspapers.

She raised all these issues with the Minister of Justice. As for the warder with the swastika, she told the Minister that she intended to raise this in parliament, a threat that succeeded in getting the man removed. Mandela sent a message to thank her for this. In her usual meticulous fashion, she wrote to the Minister after the visit to say that PAC leader Robert Sobukwe's enforced segregation was beginning to tell on him. She asked for him to be allowed more visits from his wife and for the authorities to help with her travel expenses from Johannesburg.

She addressed complaints from prisoners about the food, which she urged should be improved. Clothing was not adequate for the winter months.

Prisoners were not allowed to have photographs of their families.[5] Recreational facilities were inadequate. Hot water was not provided. Deprivation of tobacco was another hardship. She objected to the grading of prisoners by the prison authorities, in terms of the privileges they might receive.

She also raised objections to the lack of study facilities. Neville Alexander, a long-term prisoner and, later, a distinguished academic and co-author of the 1988 film *Robben Island, Our University*, had complained about the discouragement of those prisoners attempting to study. The authorities were failing to educate those who were illiterate, despite the fact that prison regulations laid down that prisoners should be encouraged to study.

As Helen Suzman observed later, 'things were bad then in the prison. They thought conditions had to be as tough as possible, as further punishment. Some of the warders were really Nazis.' Neville Alexander saw her visit to the island as marking a turning point in the treatment of prisoners by the authorities, which was characterised at the time by severe brutality. Had she not come, in his opinion, 'there is no saying what might have happened'.[6]

It was seven years before she was permitted to visit

Robben Island again. In October 1974 she wrote to Jimmy Kruger that she could not take seriously the claim (by the prison authorities) that she 'upset the prisoners' when she visited them: 'I have ample evidence that, on the contrary, my visits in the past have had a calming effect in giving hope that there will be an improvement in conditions.'[7]

She found that the island remained a most desolate place, but that some of the practical improvements she had argued for had been put in place. The prisoners were no longer required to do hard labour. In 1980 the new Minister of Police, Louis le Grange, announced that undergraduate studies, which had been banned by Kruger, would again be allowed in the prisons and that the prisoners could receive newspapers. Both of these concessions were things for which she had been campaigning for years. She was permitted to make a further visit to the island, where she found Mandela's spirit entirely unbroken.

On one of her visits to Robben Island, according to Nelson Mandela, he pointed out to her that the Afrikaner rebel leader Christiaan de Wet had been released before having completed his six-year sentence for committing treason during the 1914 Afrikaner rebellion. Helen Suzman observed that the two cases were different. 'The government could afford to release De Wet because his rebellion had been crushed. Yours is in the future.'[8]

Visiting Robben Island again in 1982, by which time Mandela had been transferred to Pollsmoor prison, she found the library well stocked with books by the anti-apartheid writers Alan Paton, Athol Fugard and André Brink. But the ANC prisoners told her that their current favourite reading was *Burger's Daughter*, Nadine Gordimer's 1979 novel based on the life of Bram Fischer. When Suzman told Gordimer, who was a great friend of hers, that she was now the 'pin-up' of the Robben Islanders, the novelist was delighted.[9]

When one of the prisoners complained to her that he had been assaulted, a guard came running up to her to say: 'Ah, it was really nothing, Mrs Suzman, it was only a kick up the arse!'

In the same year, she made strenuous efforts to secure the release from detention of Pravin Gordhan, then a leading ANC activist in Natal. In the democratic era, the highly respected Gordhan served as head of the South African Revenue Service (SARS) and later joined the cabinet as Minister of Finance.[10]

In April 1983 Helen Suzman received an alarming

letter (see page 198) from Winnie Mandela, who said that she had visited Mandela in Pollsmoor and had come away distressed. She said that Mandela had gone through a litany of complaints, saying that his treatment was the same as it had been on Robben Island when he first arrived there. She was concerned because 'Nelson never complains . . . you are the only one who can think of what should be done'. Articles started appearing in the British press alleging that the prison authorities were treating him badly and trying to break his spirit.

Helen Suzman used Winnie's letter to pressure the Minister of Justice, Kobie Coetsee, to allow her to visit Mandela in Pollsmoor. She had an hour-long meeting with Mandela and met Walter Sisulu and his other senior colleagues. She inspected the exercise yard and confirmed that they had access to a small library. The prison was bleak, but, she found, the food, medical attention and access to newspapers had improved, and many prisoners were studying by correspondence through Unisa. She wrote to Winnie Mandela to say that Mandela and his fellow prisoners were in good health and good spirits and that the relationship with the commanding officer seemed cordial.

In a subsequent article in the *Washington Post* she

wrote: 'There is no mistaking the aura of leadership that surrounds Nelson Mandela.' He was 'totally in charge of his situation in the prison'. As she had said on leaving Pollsmoor, she regarded him as 'our last hope'. She found that Mandela and his colleagues missed the companionship of their fellow prisoners on the island. The exercise yard had high walls and all they could see was the sky. She intended to press for them to be transferred to a more open prison. She did not believe that the authorities at Pollsmoor were trying to 'break Mandela's spirit, an aim that anyway would be unlikely to succeed with that indomitable man'.[11]

Her most comprehensive discussion with Mandela took place at Pollsmoor in May 1986. She took a parliamentary colleague, Tian van der Merwe, with her. Prison conditions had greatly improved by this time, and Mandela had access to all the newspapers. He said that he was ready to negotiate with the government and that he wanted to help to 'normalise' conditions in South Africa. Chief Buthelezi, leader of the Zulu movement Inkatha, should be involved in the negotiations. Mandela said that he was a practising Christian and an African nationalist, but he was not prepared to split the ANC because some of its members were communists. He would only accept his freedom unconditionally and if his fellow prisoners were released with him. (PW Botha by this stage was indicating that Mandela could be released if he renounced violence; Mandela's response was to call on the government to renounce violence.) He approved of the renamed Progressive Federal Party's performance in parliament and wanted them to remain there.

She came away, as always, impressed by Mandela's dignity and reasonable attitude. Despite all the years in prison, he retained a sense of humour, was not at all embittered and clearly had outstanding leadership qualities. 'There was nothing deferential in his relationship with the prison authorities … One might have expected the long, dreary, wasted years of incarceration to have worn down his spirit. Not so; and I was convinced that he was the one man who would have the will and the authority to persuade the ANC and the government to suspended violence, and who could create the climate for negotiation.' She said as much to the press, to the annoyance of the government. Kobie Coetsee phoned her, bellowing that she had broken their agreement by issuing a statement about her meeting with Mandela.[12]

It was another two years before she was allowed to

see Mandela again, once at the Constantiaberg clinic, where he was recovering from surgery, and twice at the Victor Verster prison, outside Paarl, where she found him living in a warder's cottage. The warder, Warrant Officer Swart, whom Mandela had befriended and who admired him greatly, had by then been transformed into a butler, who cooked and served lunch for them. In the course of this visit, at my request, she told Mandela of Margaret Thatcher's efforts to get him released from jail.

Helen Suzman found that, whatever differences they had over sanctions and disinvestment, the senior ANC leaders never forgot her visits and all that she had tried to do for them in prison. When, on a visit to Lusaka, she was criticised by a young ANC militant for serving in the apartheid parliament, she turned to Steve Tshwete, a leader of the military wing of the ANC and an ex-Robben Islander, to ask what difference she had made from his point of view. His response was to envelop her in an enormous bear hug.[13]

As she observed at the time, throughout her parliamentary career she had intervened on behalf of many people whose political views were radically different to hers. She was surprised at the hostility and even resentment her political stance provoked.

Nevertheless, she was in a position to help them, and help them she did.[14]

With Nelson Mandela she formed a special bond, well before he became the world's most famous political prisoner. However, she also made a huge effort on behalf of another prominent victim of detention and banning orders – Winnie Mandela. Nelson Mandela's second wife was detained and held in solitary detention for 17 months, and then banished, from 1977 to 1985, from her home in Soweto to the miserable township outside Brandfort in the Orange Free State.

Helen Suzman visited Winnie three times, making the long and lonely journey to Brandfort, dogged by the security police, who raided the house on each occasion she was there. The closeness of the two women's relationship is illustrated by the correspondence carefully preserved in the Helen Suzman papers in the William Cullen Library. In July 1978 she received a letter from Winnie, beginning 'My dear Helen' and ending 'With much love', asking for her help in avoiding being dispossessed of her house in Soweto and about money worries. Helen Suzman replied that she was 'not in very good odour' with the government, but she would try to see the Minister of Justice on Winnie's behalf.[15]

Winnie thanked Suzman for her continuing concern, noting that her letter had been opened by her 'guardians', who had not even bothered to observe the 'crude courtesy' of resealing it. She lamented the difficulty of bringing up her daughter Zindzi in such circumstances and advised against bothering the Minister as the security police intended to keep her in Brandfort as long as they wished. She was mistaken on this point, as Helen Suzman's interventions on her behalf did in the end have an effect.

On 14 January 1983 Helen Suzman described in the *Washington Post* one of her visits to Brandfort, 'a dreary little one-horse town in the middle of the veld'. On her previous visit, she observed, their conversation had been interrupted by a security policeman, who had rejected Suzman's permit to visit as invalid, and threatened to arrest Winnie if she did not leave within five minutes. They continued their conversation walking up and down the dusty street outside. Winnie still was not allowed to see more than one person at a time.

On her next visit, Helen Suzman found on arrival that, once again, there was a reception committee of security policemen searching the house. This led to some frank exchanges between her and the police while they confiscated books, pictures and a 'subversive' bedspread in ANC colours. She and Winnie laughed together when the police left, but this had long since ceased to be a laughing matter. As this episode also featured in the *Washington Post* article, US Senator Paul Tsongas and leading Congressman Stephen Solarz clubbed together to buy Winnie a new bedspread in ANC colours, which Helen Suzman duly delivered to her in Brandfort. In April, Winnie wrote to congratulate her on serving the people for 20 years (see page 198). It was a remarkable performance, a tremendous inspiration and a lesson in perseverance: 'I can assure you I am taking notes.'[16]

At Winnie's request, Helen Suzman tried unsuccessfully to get permission for a clinic to be built at the site of her house in Brandfort. Winnie Mandela asked for her help in buying the lease of her house in Soweto, which Suzman had succeeded in dissuading the local authorities from taking away from her.

In 1984, they were invited jointly to receive an award for human rights from two Scandinavian newspapers. Winnie was refused a passport, but her daughter Zenani accompanied Helen Suzman to receive the award. There was a lot of hostility from ANC exiles attending the ceremony, who did not regard a white liberal as an ally in the struggle against apartheid.[17] But this was never the attitude of Nelson or Winnie Mandela. In 1985, dedicating a book about her, *Part of My Soul Went with Him*, to Helen Suzman, Winnie Mandela wrote: 'We salute our dearest friend Helen. One day the nation will honour your tremendous work, your fight for human rights. You've always been truly one of us.'[18]

In the following year, Winnie Mandela was asked by the BBC what she thought of Helen Suzman. She said that they disagreed a lot on political issues. But she and all her people valued her role. In the early years of apartheid, without Helen Suzman there would have been no political opposition to the racist regime. 'She occupied a position of being a spokesman for all the non-voters in the country.' She went to Robben Island when conditions were extremely difficult for the prisoners. 'Had it not been for her one voice in Parliament all those years, the rest of the world would never have known what was going on in this country.'[19]

When Winnie Mandela was charged and convicted, in 1991, of involvement in a case of kidnapping and fatal assault on a young Sowetan by members of her 'football team', who were engaged at the time in a reign of terror in Soweto, Helen Suzman offered to appear on Winnie's behalf to testify to how much she had suffered at the hands of the apartheid regime. At a time when many others were seeking to ostracise Winnie Mandela, Helen Suzman was not prepared to abandon their long-standing friendship. On Helen Suzman's 90th birthday, Winnie Mandela was still paying tribute to her 'wonderful faithful loyal friend', honoured by every black South African whose life she touched.[20]

Helen Suzman's parents, Samuel and Frieda Gavronsky. *(By kind permission of the Suzman family)*

Getting married to Moses Suzman, 1937. *(Suzman family)*

Helen Suzman with the 'Race Classification' document, 1959. *(Barnard Center for Research on Women, 1959)*

Addressing a protest meeting, 1962. *(PictureNet)*

HF Verwoerd (8 March 1951), John Vorster (4 January 1978) and PW Botha (4 August 1985) – 'as nasty a trio as you could encounter in your worst nightmares'. *(Getty Images; PictureNet; Gallo Images)*

With Max Borkum at a Progressive Party rally, 1966. *(David Goldblatt/Africa Media Online)*

In her campaign office. Unpublished photo taken for *Time* magazine. *(Helen Suzman papers, William Cullen Library, University of the Witwatersrand)*

The sad harvest of apartheid. Unpublished photo taken for *Time* magazine. *(Suzman papers)*

With Chief Mangosuthu Buthelezi and Colin Eglin, on her 21st anniversary in parliament, 4 June 1973. *(Cape Argus/Independent Newspapers)*

Visiting Meadowlands High School, Soweto, 10 February 1977. *(World/Times Media Group)*

With Irene Menell, 1 July 1978. *(PictureNet)*

'Dear Helen – Here is a photograph of you intimidating the police again. Regards, Brian [Pottinger]'. *(Sunday Times/Times Media Group; Suzman papers)*

Progressive Federal Party MPs taking the oath in parliament, while being glared at by PW Botha, 1984. *(Cape Argus/Independent Newspapers)*

At KTC squatter camp, outside Cape Town, with Ken Andrew. *(John Rubython, Suzman papers)*

With Winnie Mandela in Orlando West, Soweto, 8 August 1986. They had just been detained for half an hour during a visit to a neighbouring school. *(Associated Press)*

A hug from Mandela,
26 February 1990. *(PictureNet)*

With FW de Klerk. *(Suzman papers)*

13 June 1996. *(PictureNet)*

Chapter VI

Mrs Rosenkowitz and her sextuplets

In the run-up to the 1974 general election, Helen Suzman told Colin Eglin that, if the Progressive Party again failed to win any seats other than hers, she would resign. The enormous strain of representing her party alone in parliament was becoming impossible to bear.

She described 24 April 1974 as, politically, the most exciting night of her life. The Progressive Party won five other seats, including that of Colin Eglin in Cape Town. On one occasion in parliament, when a

National Party MP accused Eglin of being unpatriotic, she took pleasure in contrasting Eglin's service in the South African Army during the Second World War with the activities of Nationalists engaged in sabotaging the war effort at the time.

The new star of the party was the charismatic Frederik van Zyl Slabbert, a former Professor of Sociology at Wits and a lecturer at Stellenbosch University, who was elected in Rondebosch. Shortly afterwards, the party won a further seat in a by-election in Cape Town, bringing Dr Alex Boraine into their team. The party's years in the wilderness were over, though the National Party remained as dominant as ever. Now the Progressives were able to allocate to other capable members most of the subjects that she had been obliged to deal with on her own throughout her 13 solitary years. It transformed her life to have friends with her in parliament to talk to, laugh and eat with and have a drink with. When she walked proudly into the House with her six new colleagues to take the oath at the opening of parliament, they were greeted by a Nationalist MP exclaiming: 'There comes Mrs Rosenkowitz' (a reference to a Cape Town woman who had recently given birth to sextuplets).

By this time she had become as well known

internationally as she was in South Africa. One day, at a lunch in Mauritius, she found herself being stared at by a hard-bitten South African woman. Expecting a harangue on politics, she was surprised instead to hear: 'Aren't you Helen Gavronsky from Germiston? And what have you been doing since then?'[1]

She was in the United States, receiving an honorary doctorate from Harvard University, when the Soweto uprising began on 16 June 1976. The Minister of Justice, Jimmy Kruger, accused her of being away 'receiving a degree from some obscure university'. In parliament she had warned the government that things were reaching a crisis point in Soweto, and had told them over and over again that, if peaceful protests were banned, and there was no improvement in the conditions of the black people in the urban areas, violent confrontation was inevitable. The expected radicalisation of young urban black South Africans had now taken place, with some of their leaders adopting what she regarded as the absurd and self-defeating doctrine of 'liberation before education'. There were violent confrontations with the police, and pupils in some cases resorted to burning down their own schools. The days of patient submission were over. She was a regular visitor to Soweto and was in touch with most of the black leadership there, visiting leading figures like Dr Ntatho Motlana and the outspoken journalist Percy Qoboza when they, too, were detained without trial.

In 1976 the Progressive Party merged with the Reform Party, which was based in Natal and led by Harry Schwarz, and was renamed the Progressive Federal Party (PFP). In party meetings, she clashed frequently with Schwarz, who was far more conservative than her. She was embarrassed by his hawkish support for the South African Defence Force (SADF).

In 1977 she addressed a mass meeting of students in the Great Hall at Wits University. To her fury, the secretary of the National Union of South African Students (NUSAS) urged the students to boycott the whites-only elections without, in her view, offering any credible alternative course of action. This she regarded as the worst kind of futile gesture and was characteristically uncompromising in saying so.[2]

A Nationalist newspaper, *Die Transvaler*, printed with glee an article claiming that she had been chased out of one of the schools she had been visiting in Soweto. The report was the reverse of the truth – she had, in fact, been cheered by the students – and the Press Council required the paper to print an apology.[3]

In fact, she continued to a receive a rousing reception at high schools in Soweto. For these visits, Kruger (whom she described as 'a nasty little bully') threatened to prosecute her under the Riotous Assemblies Act. On meeting her in a lift in the government building, he snarled, 'I will get you', receiving in return a few choice epithets from her. The purpose of her visits to Soweto was in fact to persuade the pupils to return to school, rather than listening to the activists advocating liberation before education.

In January 1977, during a no-confidence debate in parliament, she denounced the methods of riot control used by the South African Police, calling once again for the police to be given proper equipment and to be trained in the use of non-lethal methods, rather than firing live ammunition into crowds. Nothing, she concluded, had been learned from the lessons of Sharpeville. Violence had become endemic in South Africa, with police violence making a major contribution to it. The people of Crossroads, an informal settlement outside Cape Town, were telling her that, if the police were kept away, the violence there would end.

In February, the black American ambassador to the United Nations, Andrew Young, was quoted as saying: 'Mrs Helen Suzman is the only South African I can't get along with. I can deal with cold hatred but I can't stand paternal liberalism.' She was absolutely furious, particularly as she had only ever met him once, at a group breakfast in Washington. 'Evidently', she declared, 'I am not at my best at breakfast.' Young had to make an abject apology. 'I regret that my comments were misinterpreted as I have long admired Mrs Suzman, and I hold her in high regard for her forthright stands on South Africa's racial problems ... Her courageous and lonely stand in the face of bitter personal and political attacks has earned her well deserved admiration. I have clarified my views ...'[4] She had resented his statement the more since, as she said, she could never be accused of paternalism: 'I have always been just as nasty to blacks as I am to whites, and that can be very nasty indeed!'[5] She meant that she could be just as troublesome to black *politicians* and made good on the promise in her efforts to hold ANC leaders just as accountable for their actions and statements as she had the leadership of the National Party.

In 1977 the United Party finally expired. In the general election in November that year, the PFP at last fulfilled her dream of becoming the official opposition, winning 17 (still only 10 per cent) of the parliamentary seats. Those elected included her friend Zach de Beer, formerly a senior executive with the Anglo American Corporation.

When parliament resumed, she voted against the replacement of Colin Eglin as leader of her party (a position she never sought herself) by Van Zyl Slabbert. She regarded Van Zyl as a relative newcomer and was not sure that he intended to remain in parliament, as he also was being considered for a senior post at the University of Cape Town. Also, she felt that Eglin was being unfairly treated. Van Zyl Slabbert, as she acknowledged, proved to be a charismatic, energetic and successful leader of the party over the next several years.

When she first visited Robben Island, the most famous prisoner there was not Nelson Mandela, but Robert Sobukwe. She found that Sobukwe was not allowed to have contact with any other prisoners. She raised his case in every subsequent year in parliament, protesting at the indefinite continuation of his detention, and helping to get permission for his family to visit him. She saw him again in the Groote Schuur hospital in Cape Town, where he was admitted suffering from terminal cancer. She was impressed by his quiet dignity, calm and thoughtful appraisal of the political situation, lack of bitterness and dismay at the deterioration in race relations resulting from the government's intransigence.

In March 1978, she attended his funeral at Graaff-Reinet. Sobukwe's wife, Veronica, had asked her to deliver an address. But, on arrival, she and her colleagues were told that the young black PAC members who had taken over the funeral arrangements did not want any whites involved, not even Sobukwe's close friend Benjamin Pogrund, of the *Rand Daily Mail*. Suzman and the Pogrunds nevertheless eventually were invited to the platform, where they found the Inkatha leader, Chief Buthelezi. When the young black pallbearers caught sight of Buthelezi, a near riot broke out and he had to be hustled off the stage. Feelings among the young comrades were running high against him as a homeland leader. It was an example of the increasing radicalisation of black youth, but it took some time for Buthelezi to forgive her for mentioning the incident to the press. She noted that it was only after Sobukwe was arrested and his organisation banned that the PAC abandoned the policy of non-violence that its leader had long advocated.[6]

In the same year, she was honoured when Alan

Paton, author of *Cry, the Beloved Country*, dedicated to her his latest book, *Save the Beloved Country*. She observed that, four years before, they had split the liberal vote by both being nominated for the chancellorship of Wits University, thereby allowing a third candidate to succeed instead. 'We both belong,' she added, 'to an endangered species – the South African liberal under attack on two fronts – from the right, as always, for being "sickly humanists" and on the left, in recent years particularly, for eschewing radical solutions for South Africa's manifold problems.' They shared, together with 'hundreds of thousands – maybe millions – of South African of all races values we hold to be sacrosanct – simple justice, equal opportunities, maintenance of civil liberties and the rule of law'.[7]

As the National Party celebrated its 30th year in power, she pointed to the country's increasing isolation, greeted, as she put it, by 'an indignant wail of self-pity'. The result of the government's policies was, increasingly, militant black resistance. 'These are some achievements – if you have a death wish!'[8]

At a protest meeting at Wits University she said that she had witnessed 'law after law passed to control our lives in tight racial compartments to regulate from the cradle to the grave every facet of life for blacks in this country' and the ever-increasing powers taken by the Minister of Police to lock people up without trial and subvert all the democratic processes of the law. Yet even she had been shocked by the ways in which 'our idiot leaders' went ahead with police attacks on Crossroads, which she knew well from her many visits there.

The 1979 session of parliament was dominated by the Information Scandal and by the revelations, despite ministerial denials, that the Department of Information, led by Dr Connie Mulder, had used taxpayers' money to finance a pro-government newspaper, *The Citizen*. The director general of the department also had tried to buy the *Washington Times* newspaper and to gain control of the major independent South African newspaper group. The scandal led to the resignation of Mulder and to the prime minister, John Vorster, being ousted by the even more authoritarian Minister of Defence, PW Botha (though Vorster was kicked upstairs for a while to serve as president).

'Towards the end of his regime,' Helen Suzman wrote in her memoirs, 'Vorster had had a bellyful of me.' He turned nasty and sarcastic in their acrimonious exchanges in parliament. PW Botha had long been her particular *bête noire*, and was someone with whom she had a 'singularly hostile relationship'. In one previous parliamentary exchange, he had told her to 'stop chattering ... If my wife chattered like the Hon. Member, I would know what to do with her ... She is like water dripping on a tin roof.'[9] Helen Suzman's response was that, if he were a woman, 'he would arrive on a broomstick!'

To Botha's irritation, she kept reminding him that he had masterminded the forced removal of the 30,000 inhabitants of District Six in Cape Town, to the outrage of the entire coloured community. She also recalled his hostility towards South African soldiers serving with the Allied forces during the Second World War. In the course of an all-night debate, Botha observed: 'The Hon. Member for Houghton, it is well known, does not like me.' 'Like you? I cannot stand you!' was her response.[10] He accused her of going to America to receive an award from South Africa's enemies, the honour being a human rights award from the United Nations.

Helen Suzman had long suspected that the government had been intercepting her mail. In mid-1979 this was confirmed to the *Observer* in Britain by a defector from the Bureau of State Security (popularly known as BOSS). She told the press that the one comforting thought about the surveillance was that, when tapping her telephone, the government at least must have heard some home truths about themselves, 'often couched in good Anglo-Saxon terms'. PW Botha's response was to say: 'The Hon. Member is a vicious little cat when she is wronged, but I say to her: "Choose your friends better."'[11] This was backed up by the claim that she had entertained an American 'spy', who had been permitted to use her notepaper. The 'spy' turned out to be an American academic, Professor Robert Rotberg, who had stayed with her in Johannesburg. His published conclusions were that there was no prospect any time soon of a successful revolution in South Africa, nor was there much prospect of a positive evolution on the part of the government.

She attacked the whitewash findings of the commission set up to inquire into the 1976 Soweto uprising, pointing out that 114 people had been killed by the police in the first six days and 445 in the period covered by the report. She later also attacked the police for the infamous 'Trojan Horse' incident in October 1985 in the Cape Town suburb of Athlone, when hidden police jumped up from the back of a truck to shoot at demonstrators. The supposedly reformist Minister for Constitutional Development and former South African ambassador to the United States, Dr Piet Koornhof, also known as 'Piet Promises', meanwhile, kept warning the opposition not to raise expectations among black people that, he contended, could not be realised.

On 5 February 1982, the detained trade unionist Dr Neil Aggett was found hanged in his cell at the police headquarters in John Vorster Square in Johannesburg. Helen Suzman had received allegations from another prisoner that Aggett had been badly mistreated – kept naked, made to stand for hours and beaten. As the case was *sub judice*, she was not supposed to debate it in parliament. To overcome this, she proceeded to make a detailed statement about reports she had received from other inmates of the appalling ill-treatment meted out to a vulnerable prisoner, only revealing at the end of her statement that the prisoner in question had been Neil Aggett, releasing her statement in advance to the press.

Along with 1,500 other people, she attended Aggett's funeral service in Johannesburg, on 13 February. At the inquest, her friend George Bizos named two security policemen who he demanded should be charged with culpable homicide, after calling ten former detainees to testify about Aggett's treatment under interrogation. The detainee who had contacted her gave evidence. Yet the magistrate, PAJ Kotzé, in an absolute travesty of justice, ruled that the police could not be held responsible for his death.

Helen Suzman stated in parliament that the magistrate's finding in the Aggett inquest was outrageous. Kotzé had dismissed the evidence of every detainee and accepted that of every security policeman. Far from disciplining the security policemen involved, Colonel Piet Goosen, notorious from the Biko case, had been promoted. The Helen Suzman papers include a letter dated 23 September 1982 from the family of Neil Aggett, thanking her for passing on to them a generous contribution given to her for their legal expenses by an anonymous donor, and for her continuing efforts in the case.[12]

Following the ruthless treatment of squatters in the Nyanga township, near Cape Town, at the hands of the police, she interceded on behalf of a large group of demonstrators to avoid a clash with the police in Cape Town (including the police dog incident described in the Introduction). Her reward was to be accused of taking part in an illegal procession, with PW Botha snarling at her: 'You try to break the law and you will see what happens to you,' causing her to snarl back: 'I am not afraid of you. I never have been and I never will be. You have been trying to bully me for 28 years and you have not succeeded yet.'[13]

Her campaign continued on behalf of the people in the huge informal settlements around Cape Town. Whenever they heard of a police raid, she and her colleague Ken Andrew would drive out to settlements like Crossroads in an attempt to curb police action. They finally helped to extract an announcement from Koornhof that a new township for black people would be constructed at Khayelitsha. Crossroads periodically erupted in serious violence, causing her to say in parliament that 'Nothing has been learned from the lessons of Sharpeville and Soweto ... We saw police, absolutely unprotected, standing in the street, shooting at crowds who were throwing stones at them.'[14]

In March 1984 she went to Nkomati on the Mozambique–South Africa border to witness the signing of an agreement between President Samora Machel of Mozambique and the South African government. As she wrote to her daughters, Mozambique was on its knees, destabilised by South Africa's support for the Renamo rebel movement, which contributed to a full-scale civil war in that country.

She sat next to the Commissioner of Police, who gave her a 'glib spiel about the need to win the hearts and minds of the people'. She was reminded of President Lyndon Johnson's saying: 'When you've got them by the balls, their hearts and minds will follow.' That was what had happened to Mozambique. Machel had little option but to accept South Africa's demands, among which were that Mozambique cease to allow the ANC to operate from its territory. Her scepticism was justified as, despite the Nkomati Accord, the conflict continued, and so did covert South African military support for Renamo.[15]

She paid a visit to the operational area on the Namibia–Angola border, accompanied by General Constand Viljoen, head of the SADF. She found the Ovambo population supporting the South West African People's Organization (SWAPO) and concluded that they would win any free election, whenever one was held. Aware that South African troops were operating deep inside Angola, she warned Louis le Grange about the dangers of getting involved in a war there, countering his arguments with: 'Yes, but your northern border, my dear, is not inside Angola.'[16]

John Battersby, then political correspondent of the *Rand Daily Mail,* describes her modus operandi during this period, recalling her regular visits to the morning editorial meeting 'with advance Roneoed copies of her speeches in her neat and consistent hand. As a journalist they were like manna from heaven because you knew Helen was always going to say something worthwhile and the headline was not hard to find. She would set the sparks flying in the House and the place would come to life when she got up to speak.'

When she was nominated for the Nobel Peace Prize in 1981, she said that she did not see how she deserved it for simply doing her job. In her view it should go to the Solidarity leader Lech Walesa, as it did.[17] She was nominated again in 1982, and again in 1984, when the prize was awarded to Archbishop Desmond Tutu, who said that he would have been happy to share it with her.

On her visits abroad, she did not take kindly to being harassed by activists several thousand miles from the front line for being 'part of the system'. On a visit to New York, she was surprised to be told that a demonstration was being organised against her by BOSS. This turned out to be a group of 'Black

Soul Sisters', who got short shrift when they tried to interrupt a speech she was making at Barnard College. Another speaker was corrected by her when she claimed to have just visited Soweto and found it entirely surrounded by barbed wire. On a visit to Australia, she was unimpressed by the performance of an ANC spokesman who talked what she regarded as 'the usual rubbish about instant revolution'.[18]

Chapter VII

She had fought the government tooth and nail

In 1983 the Botha government proposed a new constitution for South Africa, based on a three-chamber parliament, to be elected separately by white, coloured and Indian voters. This was presented by the government, and accepted by the great majority of the white electorate at the time, as a major step forward. The new constitution was opposed fiercely by Helen Suzman and her colleagues in the PFP because of the exclusion of the black majority, which represented 70 per cent of the population, and because of the racially exclusive nature of the proposed tricameral parliament. She predicted, correctly, that this 'reform', regarded by many PFP supporters as being 'a step in the right direction', would make things worse, not better. The English-speaking press generally supported the proposals, except for the *Star*, which urged its readers to abstain from voting, causing her to quote sardonically a notice in the newspaper's office: 'the Editor's indecision is final!' The government's proposals were approved by a two-thirds majority in a referendum of the white electorate only.

A direct outcome of the campaign was the formation of the United Democratic Front (UDF), bringing together a host of civic organisations and trade unions closely aligned with the ANC. In the elections to the tricameral parliament, which was opposed by the UDF, there were low turnouts in the coloured and Indian communities. Through constant demonstrations, rent boycotts and other forms of 'mass action', the UDF set about making the townships ungovernable.

In the Delmas treason trial, which began in October 1985 and lasted until December 1988, 22 UDF activists, including Mosiuoa 'Terror' Lekota and Popo Molefe, were accused of terrorism and subversion. Helen Suzman attended sessions of the trial, as did

I on my arrival in South Africa as British ambassador. When eventually the accused were acquitted on appeal in 1989, I introduced them to the British Foreign Secretary, Douglas Hurd, who was visiting South Africa and who found them firmly committed to negotiations on a new constitution. Post apartheid, Lekota became premier of the Free State and then served as Minister of Defence. He later became a critic of the ANC, and in 2008 led a breakaway to form a rival party, the Congress of the People (Cope).

In March 1985 the police shot and killed 20 people in Langa township in Uitenhage in the east of the Cape province. The demonstrators had been marching to the funeral of victims of police shootings a few days before. In parliament, Helen Suzman disassembled the police account of what had happened, repeating the plea she had often made before: 'Keep the police away from funerals, especially those of people who have been killed by the police.'[1] Live ammunition was supposed to be used only as a last resort. At Uitenhage, it had been used instead as a first resort. A subsequent inquiry showed that many of those killed or injured had been shot in the back.

In the same session she introduced a motion in parliament on civil liberties, urging that South Africa should return to the rule of law. This time a *verligte* National Party MP, Leon Wessels – later to become a cabinet minister under De Klerk – paid tribute to her as a 'noteworthy political opponent'. She had, he observed, fought the government tooth and nail. 'We on our side wish to give her credit for that.'[2] The Minister of Law and Order, Louis le Grange, said that it had been hard to endure her for the past 32 years. 'Go to Northern Ireland … We will give you an exit permit.'

Yet Le Grange was always correct in his dealings with her, unlike his predecessors, Vorster and Kruger. When he became Speaker, he was friendly to her, allowing her to speak whenever she wished. During her one visit to Moscow, in 1982, when she accompanied her husband to a medical conference, she sent a postcard of the Kremlin back to Louis le Grange with the words, 'Plenty of law and order here!' When, in 1989, she was awarded an honorary knighthood (Dame of the British Empire) by the Queen he wrote to congratulate her, saying that she was a worthy recipient of the honour. In turn she thanked him for allowing her portrait to be displayed prominently in a parliamentary corridor, causing him to reply that he had always wanted to see her hanged in parliament! He told a journalist subsequently that, whenever he passed her portrait, she seemed to be looking down at him and saying: 'I told you so.'

PW Botha had no intention of abolishing apartheid, but he did set about modernising it, on one occasion declaring that South Africa had to 'adapt or die'. In doing so, he made some reforms that Helen Suzman had been demanding for many years. In 1979 the government had taken the important step, which she had advocated for two decades, of recognising black trade unions, including the right to strike. In 1985 it repealed Section 16 of the Immorality Act, prohibiting sex across the colour line, and the Prohibition of Mixed Marriages Act. Helen Suzman welcomed the repeal of these pieces of legislation, which had caused so much misery and absurdity. As she observed with grim amusement, she was starting to have to get used to listening to government ministers echoing speeches she had made many years before.

Most important of all, in her view, was the abolition in 1986 of the pass laws. More than two million people had been arrested for pass violations over the preceding decade. As she had predicted, economic forces had rendered the pass laws impossible to enforce, compelling recognition of the permanence of black South African settlement in urban areas.

During the debate in parliament, she received an accolade from another 'progressive' National Party MP, Albert Nothnagel, who observed that she 'could see further than many other people in South Africa ... although she does lash out at us at times, I hardly think there will ever again be anyone in the history of this country who could do as much for human rights as she has done.'[3] This may have been too much for PW Botha, who despatched Nothnagel to be South African ambassador to the Netherlands.

But, as it sought to modernise, so the Botha government also proceeded further to militarise the regime. The security police had long been a largely unaccountable law unto themselves, responsible for the deaths of thousands of people. In the mid-1980s, PW Botha and the security chiefs set up a clandestine organisation with the Orwellian name of the Civil Cooperation Bureau (CCB) to 'take out' enemies of the regime, which increasingly was behaving like a Latin American military junta.

Helen Suzman did everything in her power to help two well-known ANC activists who later fell victim to the regime's death squads. The activist Griffiths Mxenge was first arrested in 1966, then released, but was subjected to a banning order. She helped to get this lifted, but warned that it might be a good idea for him to go to the UK, 'judging by my past conversations with the Minister about you'. He wrote to say 'I often wonder what our country would look like without a courageous Mrs Helen Suzman', and to thank her for the manner in which she had fought his case. She helped to get him admitted as a practising attorney in Durban in 1974, only for him to be murdered by police agents in 1981.[4]

The Biko affair had confirmed her worst suspicions about the security police in the eastern Cape, where two Progressive Party colleagues and close friends of hers, Molly Blackburn and Di Bishop, were active in helping victims of the system and in engaging her support. She met the leading eastern Cape ANC activist, Matthew Goniwe, in Pollsmoor prison. She was told by Louis le Grange that 'Mr Goniwe is certainly very naive when he cannot understand why he has been locked up'. On 27 September 1984 she wrote to Le Grange appealing for Goniwe's release and asking the Minister to 'restrain himself' until November so that she would not have dozens more cases to deal with on her return from a visit overseas! On 12 October she was informed by Le Grange of his agreement to Goniwe's release, only for the activist to be murdered, with three of his ANC colleagues from Cradock, by agents of the regime. She warned her two friends to watch out for their own safety, given the 'very ugly forces at work in this country'.[5] When Molly Blackburn subsequently was killed in a car accident, Helen Suzman attended her funeral in Port Elizabeth, as did thousands of black South African mourners, all in ANC colours.

The 1980s saw increasing international support for measures, including sanctions and disinvestment, to isolate South Africa economically. In April 1985 she wrote to Simon Jenkins, editor of *The Economist*, that the campaign for disinvestment seemed to have reached tidal-wave proportions. She could understand the moral and punitive motivation, but found it difficult to believe that either sanctions or disinvestment would cause radical reform of racial policies. She considered that false parallels were being drawn with the civil rights movement in the US: 'If the situation had been 20 million whites (in power) and 200 million blacks (out of power) in the 1960s, it would have taken centuries to get the civil rights legislation through.'[6]

In August 1985 there was intense speculation about a speech PW Botha was scheduled to make to the National Party congress in Durban. This was advertised in advance, in particular by the foreign minister, Pik Botha, as heralding a major political breakthrough. A draft of the speech talked of all population groups needing to be jointly responsible for decision-making in government and ended with the words: 'Today we are crossing the Rubicon.'

This was not the speech PW Botha was prepared to deliver. Instead, in a characteristic finger-wagging performance, Botha said that he was not prepared to lead white South Africans 'on a road to abdication and suicide'.

In the *New York Times Magazine* (3 August 1986) Helen Suzman addressed the issue: what should the United States do about South Africa? If the desire to distance the United States from a morally repugnant system, and to punish South Africa for its glaring defects, regardless of the consequences, was paramount, then sanctions and disinvestment sprang readily to mind, with political expediency pointing in the same direction. The South African issue had been reduced to a simple equation in the US: 'If you are against sanctions and disinvestment, you must be a racist.' In the previous year, 28 American companies had withdrawn from South Africa. The companies that had remained in the country were doing far more to break down apartheid than those that had left. The effect of sanctions on unemployment would not be felt by those living thousands of miles away, while South Africa's neighbours remained critically dependent on the South African economy.

In October 1986 the Irish diplomat and journalist Dr Conor Cruise O'Brien was prevented by student demonstrations from delivering lectures at Helen Suzman's alma mater, the University of the Witwatersrand, and at the University of Cape Town. Academic freedom was one of the causes about which Helen Suzman cared passionately indeed. She was unimpressed by what she regarded as the feeble response of the university authorities to the blatant infringement of this principle.[7]

* * *

At the start of the 1986 parliamentary session, Van Zyl Slabbert stunned his PFP colleagues by telling them that he intended to resign from parliament and as leader of the party. Helen Suzman, appalled that the leader of the official opposition should choose to damage his party in this way, did her utmost to dissuade him. What infuriated her most of all was his statement that he had stuck it out for seven years. 'Don't talk to *me* about seven years!' she replied nastily.[8] He said he believed that extra-parliamentary politics were more meaningful to the country.

Alex Boraine resigned in his wake to help Slabbert found the Institute for a Democratic Alternative for South Africa (Idasa). The institute organised a series of what she acknowledged were worthwhile conferences between Afrikaner liberals and the ANC, including a ground-breaking meeting with Thabo Mbeki and others in Dakar, Senegal, for which Slabbert was denounced by PW Botha as, in Lenin's term, a useful idiot. Following the Dakar meeting, the British and other embassies sent representatives to the airport to try to help ensure that Slabbert was not arrested or attacked on his return. Slabbert showed great courage as, living at the time on a quite isolated farm between Johannesburg and Pretoria, he obviously was a target for the security police or one of the regime's assassination squads. He believed in what he was doing, and the bridges that he, with others, was trying to build between *verligte* Afrikaners and the ANC were to prove important in the subsequent negotiations between the two sides.

Helen Suzman, however, did not forgive him for

what he had done to her party, for which she had tried so hard and so long to win support, and for what she regarded as a lack of staying power. As British ambassador to South Africa, my main task was to try to persuade the National Party and the ANC to talk to one another. Once under a neutral roof, which the embassy could help to provide, they proved to be surprisingly interested in doing just that. Trying to help achieve a reconciliation between Helen Suzman and Van Zyl Slabbert proved to be no less challenging a task. I tried arguing with her that, in an important sense, they both were right. But this was not an easy process of mending fences. When, eventually, they did get together, however, the reconciliation was complete, as she liked and admired Van Zyl, even though she thought he was naive at times about his friends in the ANC. On many of my subsequent visits to Johannesburg, the three of us had dinner together, with Jane Slabbert and the liberal editor Richard Steyn, with Van Zyl concluding that Suzman had, after all, been right about the ANC's insistence on complete loyalty to the party and distrust of those who were more independent-minded.

A consequence of Slabbert's defection was that the PFP lost seats in the 1987 general election and, to her annoyance, it was replaced as the official opposition by the ultra-right-wing Conservative Party (CP). Wits University, in an act of craven stupidity for which they were to spend the next several years apologising, refused to allow her to speak on the campus, but provided a platform for Winnie Mandela, who had just promised to liberate South Africa 'with our matches and our necklaces' (burning tyres draped around the necks of opponents). Helen Suzman's opponent in Houghton, ironically, based his campaign on a photograph of her with Winnie Mandela, using it to suggest that she had condoned what Winnie had said. In fact, Suzman had condemned it strongly. This 'black' propaganda had no effect on her ultra-loyalists in Houghton but, as she feared, did have an impact elsewhere. As a result of the disappointing election result, Colin Eglin gave way as leader again, to Zach de Beer.

In 1987, at PW Botha's insistence, Bills were drafted to reduce the autonomy of the universities and to curb campus protests by students and staff, with the government threatening to withhold subsidies if the universities did not comply. Helen Suzman and I combined forces to seek to persuade the Minister for Higher Education, FW de Klerk, not to proceed with these Bills. De Klerk told us that he had reached the same conclusion himself.[9]

Helen Suzman's last direct contact with PW Botha was in 1988, when she and Colin Eglin saw him to argue for the lives of the Sharpeville Six, who had been charged with the murder of the black mayor of Sharpeville. I had helped to persuade her of the need in this case to request a meeting with PW Botha, despite her fierce antagonism towards him. As they entered the State President's office, Colin Eglin, conscious of the intensity of her feud with Botha, urged her to 'behave yourself – the lives of six people are at stake'. David Welsh, Professor of Politics at UCT, had reminded her of a speech made by the National Party leader, DF Malan, during the Second World War, when he pleaded for the lives of two Afrikaners sentenced to death for bombing a post office to sabotage the war effort. This was the argument she deployed, effectively, in the meeting with her arch-enemy.

By prior arrangement with her, I saw Botha on the same day to tell him of the consequences for South Africa if the six were executed. I told her that the head of the Dutch Reformed Church, Professor Johan Heyns, who had declared apartheid a heresy, had promised me that he also would intervene with Botha on that day. The cumulative effect of these efforts was to persuade the normally intransigent Botha to commute the sentences. It was characteristic of Helen Suzman that, in dealing with her most hated enemy, she found a line of argument best calculated to make an impact on him.[10]

She continued in parliament to issue the clearest warnings to PW Botha and the security chiefs about the consequences of further major cross-border raids by the SADF and other provocative actions.[11] We also combined our efforts to help to secure commutation of the death sentence of the Durban bomber, Robert McBride, to life imprisonment, though not out of any enthusiasm for the individual concerned.[12]

Helen Suzman did not regard herself as having been elected to parliament to pursue women's issues. But the large amount of material in the Suzman archive relating to the laws on divorce, abortion and matrimonial property rights is a testimony to the amount of time and effort she devoted to these. Particularly from 1975, she campaigned, in the face of often blatantly sexist resistance from the National Party and other members, to remedy the inferior status of women under South African law. She was disappointed that there was 'not a single, solitary female' in the parliamentary gallery to witness the eventual passage of the Matrimonial Property Act in 1984 and the Marriage and Matrimonial Property Law Amendment Act in 1988, but was understandably proud of the progress she had helped to achieve.[13]

At the same time, she redoubled her efforts to get the government to deal more seriously with the issue of population control, campaigning for nationwide education about birth control and liberalisation of the highly restrictive law on abortion. She understood more clearly than others that the end of apartheid would not of itself do much to deal with the problem of massive informal settlements clustered around the major cities, the never-ending influx of people from the rural areas and a population increasing at the rate of one million per annum.

Throughout her career she was the recipient of a large amount of threatening hate mail, much of it anti-Semitic or accusing her of being a communist. Some of these letters are preserved in her personal archive.[14] At her home, she received many abusive telephone calls, her method of dealing with them being to emit an ear-splitting blast on a dog whistle. When she complained to the Commissioner of Police about a persistent, late-night heavy-breathing caller, he amused her by asking if she would mind the police listening to her calls to see who the caller might be. If he consulted his friends in the security police, she observed, he would find that they had been listening to her calls for the past three decades.

Her opposition to general sanctions complicated her relationships with many people overseas and with the liberation movements, which had expected her to support punitive actions against the regime she had fought so hard and so long. Her views were expressed in her usual uncompromising fashion. She did not believe that forcing South Africa to turn in on itself was a good idea at all. What it needed was to open up to the outside world.

She regarded the disinvestment campaign as self-defeating since, as in the respective exits of Mobil and Barclays, it resulted in the disposal of their assets at fire-sale prices to local business groups. Companies that stayed, like Shell, BP, Rio Tinto and Unilever, in her view were doing far more to break down apartheid structures through equality of opportunity and the help they were giving to social projects.

She admitted rather grudgingly, as a sports enthusiast herself, that the sports embargo did bring home to white South Africans the extent of their isolation, in an area that mattered to them more than most. 'My own party,' she wrote, is not in favour of isolating South Africa in the sporting world ... I will admit, however, that the growing threat of sporting isolation is causing uneasiness among thousands of white South Africans'. In April 1971 she wrote to Lord Redcliffe-Maud, former British High Commissioner in South Africa, that 'I have got to the stage now where I think the sporting boycotts are a damn effective punitive exercise'.[15]

She did not oppose nuclear, military or oil sanctions, though she pointed out that the latter had helped to create a new oil-from-gas industry in South Africa. The embargo on military supplies undoubtedly did have an impact in preventing the SADF from modernising its equipment to the extent that the generals would have wished. When, in the mid-1980s, Chase Manhattan and other Western banks refused to roll over South Africa's debts, she regarded these market sanctions as being an inevitable consequence of the country's misguided policies and as having a substantial impact, as South Africa thereafter suffered from a significant capital outflow. But, conscious as she was of the appalling poverty and lack of job opportunities for ordinary South Africans, and the absence of any social safety net, she adamantly opposed blanket sanctions of a kind that would put tens of thousands of black South Africans out of work.

Her particular scorn was reserved for leaders like Zimbabwe's prime minister, Robert Mugabe, whose countries were more than ever dependent on the South African economy thanks to their own mismanagement, and for the former Australian prime minister, Malcolm Fraser, for advocating a boycott of South African agricultural exports that clearly would benefit Australia, while threatening the livelihoods of black and coloured South Africans. As she pointed out, every survey demonstrated that black South Africans did not support sanctions that would risk costing them their jobs. This put her at loggerheads with, among others, Archbishop Desmond Tutu, who amused her by addressing her as 'dear child', even though she was 14 years older than him. She liked and admired the Archbishop, but she considered the doctrine, prevalent at the time, that general sanctions were the only alternative to bloodshed, as self-evidently flawed. General impoverishment was bound to lead to more bloodshed, not less.[16]

She regarded the notion that the government would be overthrown by force as no less fanciful. The

SADF for many years to come was going to be more than a match for the ANC's military wing, Umkhonto we Sizwe (MK, 'Spear of the Nation'), which, as the ANC leaders acknowledged privately themselves, was engaged in what they described as 'armed propaganda'. She knew from her conversations with Nelson Mandela, who had founded the military wing in response to the utter intransigence of the government, that he shared this assessment of its actual military capabilities. The armed struggle, to him, was one of the means of getting to negotiations, not a substitute for them.

This unequal balance of forces meant that, in her view, change had to come from within the regime. The government had to be *persuaded* to give up power, and she was against actions that might inhibit that. Her conviction that this was not an impossible goal was reinforced by hearing the younger and more progressive National Party MPs, who talked increasingly in terms that bore an uncanny resemblance to the arguments she had been deploying for the past three decades.

She followed with close interest developments in the Soviet Union, understanding that the Soviet economic crisis, the country's loss of interest in Africa and the changes that were under way in Moscow could undermine fatally the ability of the so-called securocrats around PW Botha to make much further play with the supposed Soviet threat so far as South Africa was concerned. The reforms set in motion by the Soviet premier Mikhail Gorbachev opened the way for agreement on the withdrawal of Cuban forces from Angola and a political settlement at long last in South West Africa (Namibia). What South Africa needed, she observed to me at the time, was a Gorbachev of its own.

In March 1988 Harry Oppenheimer said that, whenever he was downhearted or depressed at the course of events in South Africa, he had only to think of Helen Suzman, and the battles she had fought over 35 years, to feel a renewal of faith. He paid tribute to her intellect and her grasp of economic issues. South Africa's economic potential simply could not be reconciled with the philosophy of apartheid. The government had obstinately followed a disastrous economic policy: 'And who in the long battle against all this injustice, cruelty and folly has played a part to compare with Helen's?'[17] Nor did she ever doubt the ultimate outcome of that battle. Never content to fight for a good cause and lose, she was fighting to win.

Chapter VIII

Quite inevitably, time is on our side

Helen Suzman's view of FW de Klerk, who took over as leader of the National Party when PW Botha suffered a stroke early in 1989, was fundamentally different from that of his predecessors. She always had found De Klerk to be friendly and courteous in his dealings with her. In 1974, to her surprise, she had been invited to address members of an offshoot of the Afrikaner Broederbond in De Klerk's constituency of Vereeniging. No doubt De Klerk had been behind the invitation. He introduced her in glowing terms, while making clear that their political views were very different.[1]

I shared with her the outcome of two of my own early meetings with the supposedly conservative leader of the National Party in the Transvaal. Noting that I had been involved in the Rhodesian settlement, De Klerk wanted me to know that, if he had his way, South Africa would not make the same mistake as the Rhodesians. What was the mistake, I inquired? 'Leaving it much too late to negotiate with the real black leaders,' De Klerk replied.

When Johann Rupert and I had dinner with De Klerk on the day the government sought to ban the UDF, De Klerk said that he had not been consulted and, if he had been, he would have opposed the ban.

At a lunch shortly before the opening of the 1989 parliamentary session, Helen Suzman found herself sitting next to De Klerk. He asked why people thought he was '*verkramp*'. 'Because you never make a *verligte* speech,' was her reply.

Addressing parliament for the first time as National Party leader and as Acting State President, De Klerk proceeded to make a very *verligte* speech indeed about achieving full civil rights for all South Africans, and stated that the objective must be a democratic system in which no community dominated another. In her final meeting with him on leaving parliament, she observed that checks and balances would be needed to prevent abuse of power by the majority. De Klerk said that she had become a Nat. Not at all, she replied: 'You have become a Prog.' It was consistently her view that authority should not be handed over to a majority with unfettered power.[2]

In March 1989 she petitioned the Minister of Justice for suspension of the death penalty. On 18 May she said in parliament how satisfying it had been, 'without actually saying I told you so', to be present when many of the laws that she had opposed when they were introduced were repealed, with the government using many of the arguments she had advanced in the first place. As a result of economic forces and increasing black resistance, the remaining apartheid laws were bound to be repealed in due course.

She told De Klerk that his statement of intent must be translated into reality. She saw him not as a starry-eyed liberal, but as a pragmatic, intelligent man who understood what needed to be done to secure the country's future. He had not previously had the authority to be able to do so. She quoted the African saying about not arguing with the crocodile when you are still in the water – a clear reference to PW Botha, who was known to opponents and cabinet colleagues alike as the '*groot krokodil*' (great crocodile). But now, she said, De Klerk was no longer in the water and could do what needed to be done to restore peace at home and South Africa's reputation abroad. Above all, he must use his powers to prevent all further offensive actions by the state.[3]

This was not her last parliamentary performance. Characteristically, that was reserved for her to bring a censure motion against Judge JJ Strydom, who had given an outrageously light sentence to a white farmer, Jacobus Vorster, who, with a friend, had beaten a black employee to death, after tying him overnight to a tree on his farm, for killing one of his dogs. Helen Suzman thought long and hard before bringing this action in parliament because, as the columnist Bernard Levin wrote in the *Times*, while her intentions were admirable, a leading London-based South African jurist was worried that actions of this kind could be brought by the Nationalists against judges of whom they disapproved. However, this was a case, as she told me, about which she was incandescent with rage.

The voluminous papers in the archive show just

how intensively and thoroughly she researched the case and the prior history of Judge Strydom, and how extensive her support network was. According to the highly respected anti-apartheid journalist John Battersby, Strydom had been interned for two years during the Second World War for pro-German sympathies. While serving as a judge in South West Africa, he became a highly controversial figure there for the extreme leniency of his judgments against a white man who shot and killed a black waiter outside a nightclub and against three white security guards who beat a black employee to death. These sentences were privately criticised by the head of the Windhoek Bar Council and publicly by the press in Windhoek, resulting in the transfer of the judge back to the Transvaal. They contrasted dramatically with the death sentences handed down by the judge in cases in which black Namibians had been convicted of similar crimes.

Helen Suzman started by introducing a motion to impeach Judge Strydom. This was disallowed by the Speaker, Louis le Grange. But she was able to draw on the assistance of her contacts on the Johannesburg Bar Council, which had stated publicly that the sentences imposed on Jacobus Vorster and Petrus Leonard were 'so grossly inadequate as to induce not simply a sense of shock, but one of outrage and concern'. The idea that 'such a crime could merit so trivial a punishment' was fundamentally undermining of the law.

Armed with all this ammunition and with the private help of a judge of the Appellate Division of the Supreme Court, WP Shultz, she petitioned the Speaker to allow her to bring a motion of censure against Strydom. This time, the motion could not be refused. The sentence handed down by Strydom in the Vorster case was a suspended prison term and a fine of R3,000 (US$1,380). In a devastating indictment, she had no difficulty in demonstrating that this was a gross perversion of justice; if the victim had been white, real justice would have been meted out. The Attorney General of the Transvaal, DB Brunette, was pilloried by her for seeking to justify this derisory sentence. The normally reasonable Minister of Justice, Kobie Coetsee, was pushed into a bizarre defence of the judgment, arguing that the white farmer would suffer sufficient humiliation from being obliged to pay for the upkeep of the victim's family.[4]

I have no idea what impelled Coetsee to use this absurd argument, for this was the man who had asked me to help persuade his colleagues to release Mandela and who had been described on one occasion by Helen Suzman herself as the best justice minister South Africa had had. As Coetsee puffed himself up on the front bench with pride, she added: 'Not that that's saying much!'

I did my utmost, unsuccessfully, to dissuade her from standing down at the end of the 1989 parliamentary session, as she remained full of energy and was, by far, the most effective member of parliament. One of the reasons for her decision to step down was the concern that, if she stayed on in parliament, it would be increasingly difficult for Irene Menell to succeed her as the MP for Houghton. She supported the merger of the PFP with two small parties led by Denis Worrall and Wynand Malan, both of whom had broken away from the National Party, but she disliked the troika leadership produced by the merger. She did not take kindly to suggestions that, to try to widen its appeal, the new entity should try to shed the Progressive Party image of which she was understandably proud.[5]

John Major, then British Foreign Secretary, announced at the UN that, to mark her extraordinary efforts for human rights, Helen Suzman would be appointed an honorary Dame of the British Empire.

She was amused by the title, but delighted by the honour, which she received with Mosie and Francie in a ceremony with the Queen at Buckingham Palace. To mark her retirement from parliament, Anglo American and De Beers provided funds to establish the Helen Suzman Chair of Political Economy at Wits University.

On 17 May 1989, the British prime minister, Margaret Thatcher, wrote to her to say that, in the long and difficult struggle against apartheid and towards a just society in South Africa, the contribution she had made was second to none. Suzman wrote back that, of course, she preferred De Klerk to PW Botha, but he too would have to adhere to the bottom line of maintaining white minority domination, albeit with a more intelligent understanding of the need for change.[6]

She found it amusing to read, as she put it, her own obituary notices. In a handwritten note (see page 190) sent from the Victor Verster prison on 22 May 1989, Nelson Mandela wrote:

> Dear Helen,
>   The consistency with which you defended the basic values of freedom and the rule of law over

the last three decades has earned you the admiration of many South Africans. A wide gap still exists between the mass democratic movement and your party with regard to the method of attaining those values. But your commitment to a non-racial democracy in a united South Africa has won you many friends in the extra-parliamentary movement ...

Fondest regards and best wishes to you and your family.

Sincerely,

Nelson

When, shortly afterwards, she visited Mandela in prison in July 1989, he autographed for her the book *Fear No Evil*, by the Soviet dissident Natan Sharansky, which she had lent him. The inscription read: 'For Helen – None can do more than her duty on earth. The countless tributes you received on your retirement from Parliament show that you acquitted yourself beyond words. You will always be in our thoughts. Meanwhile, we send you our very best wishes. From Nelson.'[7]

Chief Buthelezi hailed a 'great South African leader and friend'. Harry Oppenheimer wrote that

'Helen Suzman is more than a great South African. She has become a world figure. Without her, Parliament will be a different and poorer place.'

The great South African human rights lawyer, George Bizos, wrote to her that: 'The Thermopylae that you chose to define and guard was not a mountain path, but the whole doctrine of human rights … I will remember how you stuck your neck out on behalf of prisoners.' He recalled the impact she made on prosecutors and defendants alike when she walked into court to witness a whole series of treason trials. Her response was that, in Lusaka, she had met enough of the prisoners she had tried to help on Robben Island to form an old boys' association.[8]

Immediately after their release from prison in October 1989, Mandela's comrades Walter Sisulu and Ahmed Kathrada credited her with the improvements that had taken place in prison conditions (*New York Times*, 19 October 1989). As she wrote to Anthony Sampson, friend and biographer of Nelson Mandela, 'My jail bird chums remain staunchly loyal, despite my politically incorrect adherence to liberalism'. Another long-term prisoner and veteran communist, Govan Mbeki, father of Thabo, wrote to her in 1994: 'What a contribution you have made to the long struggle for the liberation of the people of this country. You deserve a hug for it!'[9]

When Helen Suzman retired as the MP for Houghton, she had hoped to be succeeded by Irene Menell, who had made a major contribution to the PFP. To her disappointment, this was not to be, as an able and ambitious young Johannesburg lawyer, Tony Leon, got himself nominated instead. Leon went on to become leader of the party and, from 1994, leader of the opposition. He was an effective debater in parliament, but was unable to broaden the party's support among non-white South Africans.

When Nadine Gordimer was awarded the Nobel Prize for Literature, in 1991, Helen Suzman commented that her friend's political views were more radical than her own. 'She does not think highly of white South African liberals,' but was intelligent enough to know that some of them had their uses in exposing, under parliamentary privilege, abuses and information that would not otherwise have been discovered. Gordimer, who was aligned with the extra-parliamentary opposition, noted that many on the left had denigrated Helen Suzman as epitomising the liberal stand they rejected:

But over the years I have observed ... that when people are in trouble she has been the one they have appealed to. She is the one everybody trusted. To her house, where in this country of frightened people behind bolts and bars, her only security is a couple of lap-dogs, people would turn up, sometimes late at night, in desperation when someone needed a passport and had been refused again, when someone was on the run or someone was detained in a place the police would not reveal ... Suzman never refused anyone her help, that I knew of. No matter how unpleasant or hostile the individual's attitude to her and her political convictions had been. I don't know exactly how to define this response.

It was not magnanimity, she concluded, but pure integrity, a quality not worn on the sleeve of 'this worldly well-dressed woman who would rather trout-fish than toyi-toyi'.[10]

Chapter IX

The struggle continues

On 8 February 1990, three days before his release from prison, Helen Suzman observed to me of Nelson Mandela that his reaction, and that of his generation, to white liberals was different from that of the younger, more radically politicised black leaders. The latter were less tolerant and saw liberal South Africans as an obstacle to the straightforward transfer of power without guarantees of a free press, freedom of the individual and a multiparty state.

Mandela's release from prison led to a series of

meetings between him and Helen Suzman that continued to the end of her life. The photographs of
them together are the most eloquent of tributes to the
affection in which he held her. Unlike so many of his
visitors, who came to worship at the shrine, this was
not Helen Suzman's style at all. She never hesitated
to say so when she thought he was mistaken, leading to
some hilarious exchanges with him. In one of my
own early meetings with him, the two of us saw him
together. He had just returned from a visit to Libya,
in the course of which he had described Muammar
Gaddafi as a great supporter of human rights. When
I attempted politely to persuade him that this was not
a particularly sensible thing to say, I was interrupted
by Mrs Suzman: 'How could you be so silly, Nelson!'
she exclaimed.

He never took these exchanges badly because he
knew how committed she was to him as, in her view,
the one leader who could reunify South Africa and
offer it the hope of a more peaceful future. She was
convinced, from all her experiences of him, that
Mandela invariably had the right instincts, as well as
extraordinary leadership qualities, whereas some of
his party from time to time did not. When Mandela
asked me to help him get the leader of the ANC Youth

League, Peter Mokaba, released from prison, only for Mokaba then to start talking about 'one Boer, one bullet', she listened with approval as I telephoned him from her house to say that Mokaba needed to be told to shut up. Mandela contended that 'the young man must have been misquoted', but we heard no more of 'one Boer, one bullet'.

We both urged Mandela not to call for any further disinvestment, advice which he accepted, and to stop talking about nationalising the banks and the mines. He observed with a smile that the policy had been adopted in the 1950s, 'and it was fashionable then!'

In June 1990 Helen Suzman wrote an article in the *Washington Post* about a televised discussion between Ted Koppel and Mandela on ABC's *Nightline* about sanctions, which the ANC were still demanding should be intensified. Sanctions against De Klerk's government, she pointed out, would serve only to strengthen right-wing opposition to his reforms. Investment in South Africa would not be helped by the ANC's commitment to nationalisation.[1]

At a lunch hosted in London in July by Douglas Hurd, she tackled Mandela about the ANC's call for the continuation of sanctions against the De Klerk government. The Labour Party representative kept trying to say that he agreed with the ANC, but was ignored by Mandela, who was listening to Helen Suzman. She ended by winning the argument, not least because Mandela found that Oliver Tambo agreed with her.

In February 1991 she was back in parliament for a ceremony, which I attended, to celebrate the hanging of her portrait in a place of honour in the parliamentary building. The Speaker, Helgard van Rensburg, described her career in glowing terms, only to be reminded by her that, before his party changed its ways, he had accused her of being unpatriotic and a subversive. She doubted whether her portrait would survive under a new ANC regime and was proven correct, as it was removed from the parliamentary gallery.[2] The picture later was rescued from the cellars, and hangs today in the Democratic Alliance meeting room.

Following De Klerk's decision in February 1990 to unban the ANC and other organisations and to release Mandela, Helen Suzman witnessed the repeal of the remaining apartheid legislation, including the Population Registration Act, the cornerstone of the entire system. Nearly 30 years before, she had told her supporters that the task of those who believed in non-racialism in South Africa was to survive, and to keep the flag of decency flying. 'Quite inevitably, time is on our side.' They could not continue their isolation indefinitely. The present belonged to the extremists. But the future would belong to those who believed in a settlement between the moderates of all races.

In 1990 she was elected president of the South African Institute of Race Relations (SAIRR). In her second presidential address, she quoted Winston Churchill: 'A policy is pursued up to a certain point: it becomes evident at last that it can be carried no further ... It sometimes happens that the same man, the same government, the same party have to execute the volte-face.'[3]

In September 1991, conscious of a need to reassure business leaders, Mandela asked Helen Suzman to arrange a lunch with a group of tycoons at which, to her amusement, 'he charmed the bloody lot of them'.

Invited to participate in the ensuing discussions on a new constitution, she was delighted to witness happening what she had been advocating for decades, namely, 'people who had just been in jail negotiating with the people who put them there'.[4] But she was cross to find that women represented just ten out of 228 delegates.

In 1994 she played an important role, as a member

of the Independent Electoral Commission (IEC), in supervising the elections that brought Nelson Mandela and the ANC to power. In doing so, she witnessed the amazing spectacle of virtually the whole of black South Africa 'waiting patiently in line to participate in the first meaningful elections in which any of them had been allowed to vote'. The turnout (88 per cent) was extremely high. The ANC did not, in her words, 'to the great relief of most people, including I might say, the ANC itself', obtain the two-thirds majority that would have enabled it to rewrite the Constitution.[5]

In 1993 the Helen Suzman Foundation was established to provide a forum for debates on public policy, and ever since has published a magazine, *Focus*, which has contained many high-quality contributions on political issues. Initially, Suzman was not very involved in the foundation, which was run entirely independently of her, but she became more so towards the end of her life. The foundation has made an important contribution to political discourse under its current chairman, Gary Ralfe, formerly head of De Beers, who accompanied Helen Suzman and Colin Eglin on their visit to other African countries in 1970, and under Raenette Taljaard and Francis Antonie as its directors.

In 1997 Colin Eglin was one of those invited to witness Mandela presenting three male South Africans and Helen Suzman with the Order of Merit at a ceremony in Pretoria. In doing so, Nelson Mandela said that he was 'honoured to bestow this significant award on four distinguished citizens of our country. In deciding on three of them I followed my head. In the case of the other, I am afraid I followed my heart. I shan't tell you who that other person is – but she gives me lots of trouble!'[6]

In November 1997 Mandela as President sent her greetings on her 80th birthday: 'Her unrelenting struggle for justice has touched the lives of millions of South Africans.' Each successive year brought further tributes from him. On 27 September 1998 he described her, to her amusement, as a 'world famous veteran freedom fighter', not a description she recognised herself. 'Fighter for freedom' and, above all, for human rights was the way she thought of herself. Mandela and his wife, Graça Machel, frequently turned up unannounced to greet her on her birthday. On 7 November 2002, she was both touched and entertained to be described by him as 'another old diehard veteran ... your place is assured in the history of this country ... Looking back from the safety of our non-racial democracy, we can even feel some sympathy for the National Party members who shared Parliament with you. Knowing what a thorn in the flesh of even your friends and political allies you can be, your forthright fearlessness must have made life hell for them when confronted by you.'[7]

In September 1998, she gave an address in Pietermaritzburg in honour of Alan Paton. She noted that Van Zyl Slabbert had asked why South African liberalism evoked such negative responses from some members of the liberation movement. What implications did this have for liberal values in the future? She recalled that she had been on the receiving end of criticism from people who accused her of giving legitimacy to an illegitimate government by sitting in parliament. She had used parliament to force the government to provide answers 'which, I might add, were freely used by my critics' and to fight on behalf of those it had imprisoned. Alan Paton had suffered the same criticism for opposing violence and disinvestment, notwithstanding his leadership of the Liberal Party, which had to be dissolved in 1968 when multiracial political parties were banned.

The new Constitution, she added, represented the triumph of liberalism in South Africa. Yet a liberal constitution could not of itself guarantee that the principles it contained would be respected. Alan Paton would be concerned at threats to the freedom of the press and the government's extreme sensitivity to criticism. Yet no one in the new South Africa had to fear being banned or having his passport confiscated, as Paton's had been. Water and electricity had been made available to many communities, as had primary health care. South Africa was no longer a pariah nation and Mandela was the most sought-after leader in the world.[8]

She was delighted that her long campaign to liberalise the law on abortion ended successfully when this reform was implemented by the post-apartheid government in 1996. This encouraged her to continue her efforts to get the new government to give a high priority to a nationwide programme of birth control. She got frustratingly little help from her normally most dependable ally, Nelson Mandela, when she tackled him on the subject. 'But, Helen, you know that we Africans love children,' he would say, causing her to snort 'As if the rest of us don't.'[9] But in due course the new government did implement a nationwide programme of the kind she and others had been advocating.

Concerned at rumours that Mandela as President might offer Tony Leon a post in government, she wrote to urge him not to do so, as it was important that there should remain a strong opposition voice in parliament. In the event, the offer was not made, though Leon subsequently became South African ambassador to Argentina.

Years before, she had observed that there was, in many Western countries, 'a fairly glib acceptance that all you have to do is ensure that there is majority rule and that solves the problem because that makes it a democratic form of government'.[10] But there were plenty of countries in which majority rule was accompanied by very oppressive governments.

* * *

On one of his frequent post-retirement visits to Helen Suzman in the small house next to the Marist school in Illovo, to which she had moved after her husband died, Mandela cheerfully asked her son-in-law: 'How do you cope with this troublesome woman?' 'With difficulty', he replied.

Her intense admiration for Mandela did not extend to his successor, Thabo Mbeki. She admired

Mbeki's intelligence and, especially, his pursuit of economic policies designed to keep South Africa out of the hands of the IMF and World Bank, and to avoid repeating the mistakes that had been made in much of the rest of Africa. But she disliked his treatment of Mandela, who told her as well as me that the only world leader who did not return his calls was his own former deputy.

She could not understand why this urbane and highly intelligent political leader became so paranoid about criticism. Above all, she was outraged at his denialism about HIV/AIDS, contesting even the reality of the disease. Apart from what she regarded as the intellectual absurdity of doing so, far more seriously, it led the South African government to fail to provide anti-retroviral (ARV) drugs to the hundreds of thousands of people whose lives would have been prolonged by treatment. The President's denialism and his health minister's incompetence seriously damaged and retarded the campaign to prevent the spread of HIV/AIDS. On this, as on other subjects, she found Mandela agreeing with her, though he was reluctant to criticise his successor in public.

When ANC spokesman Smuts Ngonyama stated that the Democratic Party, successor to the PFP, 'hated black people' and could not accept that there was a black government, she was outraged, wondering what the retired Nelson Mandela would make of this. 'Perhaps he had a soft spot for liberals like myself who helped him during his long incarceration that his successor does not share.'

The growing crisis in Zimbabwe concerned her greatly. On 6 June 2000, she wrote to the *Sunday Times* that Mbeki's 'softly softly' approach to the crisis in Zimbabwe had been ineffective. 'Mayhem and murder, gross intimidation and illegal land-grabs, are the order of the day.' In these circumstances, it was highly unlikely that free elections could possibly take place. She was outraged at the pressure then exerted on the South African observer team at the Zimbabwe elections to declare them free and fair when, manifestly, they were not. At around this time, Helen Suzman, Lord Carrington and I were banned from visiting Zimbabwe and declared 'enemies of the state' by Robert Mugabe. She regarded this as an honour, and always insisted, thereafter, on including it in her CV! Zimbabwe was another issue on which Mandela, who could not stand Mugabe, in private agreed with her.

These and other criticisms of the government and of the ANC for corruption and what she regarded as self-serving gobbledygook about 'transformation', entailing the 'deployment' of ANC loyalists to senior posts in the civil service and parastatals which they were unqualified to fill, and the hostile treatment of opposition members in parliament, inevitably brought retaliation from the Mbeki camp. In his 'ANC Today' newsletter of 8 January 2005, Thabo Mbeki recalled Oliver Tambo in his New Year address in 1971 as saying of a white liberal politician who had visited Zambia: 'This sweet bird from the blood-stained south flew into Zambia and sang a singularly sweet song: I am opposed to apartheid; I am opposed to the isolation of South Africa; I am opposed to violence; I am opposed to guerrillas … I am in favour of change; I am clearly in favour of change but determined to prevent change.' The same people, he objected, were now criticising the ANC's deployment of party cadres throughout the state machinery as blurring the distinction between the state and the party.

Whether or not this really represented what Oliver Tambo thought at the time, it was flatly contradicted by everything he ever had to say to me about Helen Suzman, and he never failed to pay tribute to the role she had played. In 1989 Tambo welcomed her with fulsome praise during the Five Freedoms Forum meeting with the ANC in Lusaka, saying that 'there are many among us who deserve a special accolade, including parliament's unfading star, the indefatigable Mrs Suzman'.[11]

Helen Suzman dismissed this episode as 'part of an attempt to airbrush the efforts of white liberals out of anti-apartheid history', as also evidenced by the lack of almost any reference to them in the Apartheid Museum in Johannesburg.[12] As this attack on her followed one on Archbishop Tutu, also for criticising the government, she felt that she was in good company. With the South African press and many of his own supporters astonished at Mbeki's outburst, it did the President far more harm than it did her.

This unpleasant episode was followed by another, two years later, when Ronald Suresh Roberts, in his authorised biography of Thabo Mbeki, *Fit to Govern*, quoted selectively from the statement she had made on behalf of the SAIRR at a conference on human rights in London in 1947. The book included an attempted defence of Mbeki's policy on HIV/AIDS. The Trinidad-born Roberts had arrived in South Africa in 1994. He was a controversial figure, having been described by a High Court judge as 'venomous, vindictive, arrogant and obsessive'.

What Helen Suzman had said in 1947 was that 'South Africa has a multiracial society, dominated ... by a minority group determined to maintain its supremacy. While the spirit of trusteeship is supposed to be the basis of policy, it is a trusteeship which operates on the assumption that the ward will never be of age ... The primitive state of the rural African is not well understood by people living outside South Africa, while the rapid development of the urban native is not comprehended by people living in South Africa. There then is our problem – guidance rather than criticism is urgently needed.'

Helen Suzman, in response, did not for a moment deny that, in 1947, she had favoured a qualified franchise based on educational qualifications as a stage on the way to full democratic rights. Liberals at the time were struggling to prevent the government removing the limited voting rights non-white South Africans at the time still enjoyed. The distinguished anti-apartheid journalist Patrick Laurence pointed out that Nelson Mandela, at the Rivonia Trial, himself had envisaged a limited franchise as a transitional step on the way to universal suffrage.

In her public reply, the 90-year-old Helen Suzman said that history would judge what difference she had made. She ended by inquiring in stinging terms exactly what contribution Suresh Roberts had made to the struggle against apartheid, commenting that she would not want anyone to think she had mellowed![13]

In South Africa's democratic Constitution, adopted by parliament in 1996, she had supported the adoption of proportional representation as necessary to ensure representation for the minority parties. However, in an interview in 2008 she regretted that a hybrid system had not been adopted to provide a link to constituencies as well, because under the constituency system MPs were more accountable to their electors.

It was characteristic of Helen Suzman that, despite the ANC's inexperience, she was not prepared to make allowances for them. She understood better than anyone the immense sacrifices many of them had made in the struggle against apartheid. Her efforts on behalf of prisoners and people in the townships had brought her together with vast numbers of ANC activists whom she had supported and admired. But, once they were in government, she was determined to hold them to exactly the same standards she had sought to apply to their predecessors. She was distressed at Mbeki's tendency in his cabinet appointments

– outside of the Ministry of Finance – to value personal loyalty more than competence, leading him to hold on to ministers who manifestly deserved to be fired.

As well as Mandela, she had a high regard for the older generation of ANC leaders, including especially Walter and Albertina Sisulu, Ntatho Motlana, Andrew Mlangeni, Kgalema Motlanthe and many others like them who, as they put it themselves, did not join the ANC to get rich, but to go to jail. She saw Mbeki, notwithstanding some serious flaws, as being a competent head of government, and was on friendly terms with his wife, Zanele. In relation to the party generally, however, she saw it as starting to bear a resemblance to the National Party in its desire to exploit its preponderant position to dispense patronage, override opposition and apply pressure on the press and the judiciary. She saw the future of democracy in South Africa as depending on those pressures being resisted. It was a source of great pride to her that she came to be regarded as a mentor to independent commentators determined to resist encroachment by the state on the hard-won freedoms entrenched in the Constitution.

In her discussions with me, Helen Suzman never doubted that apartheid would, in the end, be replaced by a fully democratic non-racial government; hence her constant admonitions to her constituents in Houghton that time was on their side. She was clear, however, that the struggle for democratic rights would not end there. She was delighted that the new South African Constitution incorporated the liberties for which she had fought so hard. In her view, however, the real test of those democratic liberties was not whether they were written into the Constitution, but whether they would be observed and whether the ruling party would avoid compromising the principles that had brought it to power.

She was concerned at the success of the SACP in colonising many of the senior positions in the ANC politburo,[14] but agreed that, so far as the black ANC leaders were concerned, there was no deep ideological commitment: they were first and foremost African nationalists. Her worry was about those within the liberation movement who had imbued from the SACP the idea of the primacy of the party over the institutions of the country. She saw the real fissure as not that between the communists, who never represented more than 1 per cent of the South African population, and the non-communists, but that between those who were firmly committed to democratic ideals and those whose instinctive response was to try to bring the press and judiciary to heel.

She was not pessimistic on this account, simply regarding it as a test yet to come. She was glad to be vindicated in her conviction that the South African press would continue to play its indispensable part in exposing incompetence and corruption, that black South Africans would demand both 'delivery' and accountability from their political leaders and that the courts would continue to play their role, despite pressures to politicise the judiciary. She regarded these principles as ones that had to be fought for over and over again, and in relation to which, much as she longed to be loved, 'I am not prepared to make any concessions whatsoever'.

For obvious reasons, given her own experience and record, she regarded the existence of a strong opposition as critical to the functioning of any stable democracy and was concerned at the enfeebled position of the opposition parties in the early years of ANC rule. She lived to see this situation correct itself, with Helen Zille at the head of the Democratic Alliance being elected mayor of Cape Town, then premier of the Western Cape, and her party starting to gain substantial non-white voting support.

She was, with good reason, intensely proud of her record. She never served in government, though she had the qualities to do so with success. She never sought the leadership of her party, though she was by far its most outstanding and effective member. She probably felt, instinctively, that this could bring with it too many compromises. She was no good at compromise: in fact, she rejected it entirely. If, as she believed, in politics there are signposts and weathervanes, then indisputably she was a signpost, pointing in the right direction for South Africa and demonstrating to a worldwide audience what one charismatic, fearless, indomitable woman could achieve in helping to keep alive in the darkest times the principles in which she believed.

Chapter X

*If she could speak truth to power then, when
it was so dangerous, we must do so now*

Helen Suzman died, aged 91, on 1 January 2009. At
her funeral in Johannesburg, on 4 January, the pallbearers included Kgalema Motlanthe, President of
South Africa; FW de Klerk, former President; Colin
Eglin, former head of the Progressive Federal Party;
and Arthur Chaskalson, former Chief Justice of the
Constitutional Court. The funeral was attended by,
among others, Zanele Mbeki and Winnie Mandela.
In his state of the nation address at the opening of
parliament, President Motlanthe declared that Helen

Suzman 'represented the values of our new Parliament in the chamber of the old'.

On 27 January, the Speaker of the National Assembly moved a motion of condolence, supported by leaders of all the political parties in parliament. This acknowledged the contribution she made to the attainment of democracy in South Africa by fearlessly fighting against the apartheid government.

Mnyamezeli Booi, chief whip of the ANC, recalled what she had meant to him and his comrades in the darkest days of the apartheid era: 'She made her contribution to society and we are very thankful for what she has done for us.' Tributes came from other sections of the house, including the PAC. Andrew Mlangeni, former Robben Islander and elder statesman of the ANC, lamented the loss of a great human being who fought singlehandedly for the rights of the oppressed. He recalled that she had warned parliament against banning the ANC. All kinds of insults had been hurled against her. Whenever their treatment in prison improved a little, they knew that she was on her way. Fearlessly, she went into the townships unescorted and mingled with the people in the squatter camps to see for herself the conditions in which they lived.

For the Democratic Alliance, Tony Leon recalled the unrivalled energy and courage with which she pursued the cause of simple justice in a hostile parliament, her distaste for political correctness and her willingness to confront the government, 'this one or the previous one', whenever it was warranted.

The tributes in parliament were followed on 1 March 2009 by a memorial celebration in the Great Hall of the University of the Witwatersrand. Helen Suzman's daughter, Frances Jowell, recalled the 'hundreds of letters, the phone calls at all hours of the day and night, and the people who turned up at our front door'. To the pleasure of her family, burying their prior disagreements, the ceremony was attended by former president Thabo Mbeki and his wife, Zanele. A warm letter of condolence from the couple honoured Suzman as 'one of the leading midwives of the democracy we enjoy today'. In the face of dire threats from Verwoerd and others, her daughter recalled, Helen Suzman had stated: 'I am quite determined to say what I want to say, when I want to say it, and to hell with the intimidation.'

Ann Bernstein, chairperson of the Centre for Development and Enterprise, declared that 'without her, much in that terrible period would have passed unquestioned'. It was her relentless questioning in parliament that had exposed the full extent of many abuses. She was inundated with requests for help from defenceless people. No plea went unanswered. Bernstein recalled going with Helen Suzman to the memorial service for Chris Hani, the ANC and SACP leader murdered in 1993 by a white extremist. The hall was full of militant young people. A marshal who recognised her hauled a young militant from his seat: 'Stand up for Mrs Suzman!'

Judge Dikgang Moseneke observed that 'the collective life of a people yields only a few genuine heroes'. She had condemned in parliament his own dispatch, while still a teenager, to Robben Island. In 1963 she had made a monumental speech of protest against detention without trial, renewing her protest every year thereafter.

Archbishop Tutu applauded the heartfelt tributes to her across the entire political and racial spectrum of South Africa. Echoing her, he said: 'We must have zero tolerance for corruption, for those who have their hands in the till ... The Nats were returned in election after election, with increased majorities. Where are they now? Those who hold power and are afflicted by the arrogance of power must know that ultimately they are going to get their comeuppance, for ultimately power is for service.'

Chief Buthelezi honoured her for her sheer zest for life and biting wit, as well as for her great role in the struggle. 'No one who met her will ever forget those piercing blue eyes full of intelligence.' Her contribution was as great as any of the other struggle heroes. 'She gave no quarter to her opponents and did not expect any from them.'

Nicky Oppenheimer celebrated this elegant woman with clear blue eyes and a razor-sharp mind facing down 'those arch-bullies' Verwoerd, Vorster and PW Botha and the baying mob behind them, 'armed only with deadly wit, a deep contempt for all they stood for, and sure and certain knowledge that she was right'. She used parliament to force into the cold light of day issues and facts that the apartheid regime would have liked to hide, demonstrating the real cost of apartheid in terms of human suffering. She never was a politician in the sense of the compromises that normally entailed. She was rather the voice of South Africa's conscience.

Mamphela Ramphele declared that 'if she could speak truth to power then, when it was so dangerous, we must do so now'. In their young democracy, won at the cost of so much sacrifice, 'why are we so tolerant of corruption, incompetence and abuse of public resources? Why are we silent in the face of a culture of impunity?'

Helen Zille, leader of the Democratic Alliance, recalled Helen Suzman as saying that what she stood for was 'simple justice, equal opportunity and human rights', and, recalled her quoting Theodore Roosevelt: 'I did what I could, where I was, with what I had.'

In memorial speeches on separate occasions, Raymond Louw, former editor of the *Rand Daily Mail*, recalled that 'this was a period when more than a hundred laws and regulations restricted press freedom'. But through her several hundred questions and speeches in the House much prohibited information, to the government's dismay, had to be released.

The writer Rhoda Kadalie described Suzman as fearless, politically incorrect and prejudicing her chances of the Nobel Peace Prize by opposing sanctions. In the new South Africa 'she could never understand why our government flirted with dictators and human rights-delinquent regimes'. She had been saddened that parliament had become captive to liberation politics and majoritarianism, with legislators implicated in one scandal after another and opposition MPs treated less well than she had been under the apartheid regime.[1]

* * *

Although marked by plenty of violence at the time, the relatively peaceful transition to democracy in South Africa was hailed in the outside world, especially in the United States, as some kind of miracle. At a time when many observers were predicting that events were heading towards civil war, Helen Suzman never lost faith in the chances of avoiding such a denouement. From the outset, she was convinced that, over time, ineluctable economic forces would overwhelm the apartheid system. She regarded apartheid as totally incompatible with, indeed the antithesis of, a normally functioning free economy. For the major South African and multinational corporations were proceeding steadily to undermine the system through their increasing need for trained non-white employees and managers. Her belief was justified when, in the 1980s, influx control and the pass laws, under which between two and three million people had been arrested over the preceding decades, had to be abandoned as simply unenforceable.

It was her determination to test any policy or dogma against what it would do for ordinary people that led her to break ranks with the overseas anti-apartheid movement and oppose economic sanctions which she believed would harm impoverished black South Africans without having a decisive effect on the apartheid regime.

She did not contest that external pressures, including various sanctions – military, nuclear, oil and financial – played their part and, despite her initial reluctance, she came to regard the sports boycott as highly effective in accelerating the development of multiracial sport in South Africa. But she did not believe that such pressures could be decisive in bringing down apartheid. The critical factor would be forceful and effective black resistance. She saw this as taking the form of increasingly assertive trade union activity, especially by the National Union of Mineworkers (NUM), led by Cyril Ramaphosa, and the success of the UDF – effectively the internal wing of the ANC – in winning political control of the townships during the mid-1980s.

She understood full well the reasons that had led Nelson Mandela and his colleagues to establish the ANC's armed wing, MK, and had indeed forecast that, given the government's intransigence, this was bound to happen. But she was sceptical about the achievements of MK and highly critical of the attacks on 'soft' civilian targets. Letting off occasional bombs in shopping malls and discothèques she saw as hardening white attitudes, rather than serving any more useful purpose. ANC leadership of the 'armed struggle' and the mystique surrounding it was critical to the movement's ability to assert the political control it established in the townships. Self-evidently, however, MK was not going to be a match for the SADF.

Therefore, if ultimate disaster was to be avoided, the ruling party had to be persuaded to negotiate with the real black leaders, led by Mandela, while there was still time. While she had no illusions that this would ever be accepted by Verwoerd, Vorster or PW Botha, she observed a progressive evolution of thinking among the younger National Party MPs and some of their *verligte* elders, such as Johan Heyns, head of the Dutch Reformed Church; Pieter de Lange, the reformist head of the Broederbond; Ton Vosloo, head of the main Afrikaans press group; Gerhard de Kock, head of the Reserve Bank; and the Rupert family.

White politics in South Africa were still marked by a high degree of tribalism. The *verligte* Afrikaners, influenced by academics like Willie Esterhuyse and Hermann Giliomee, were exploring their own options for the future, but these were leading them in the same direction as her. A raft of young National Party MPs – Roelf Meyer, Leon Wessels, Sam de Beer, Kobus Meiring and others – thought and spoke like her, and by the 1980s were moving into government.

At the same time she knew, from her own conversations with him, that Nelson Mandela did not believe in a seizure of power or in the possibility, for the foreseeable future, of overthrowing the government by force. She knew that he believed in negotiations leading to a genuinely democratic constitution.

When Helen Suzman met Margaret Thatcher at 10 Downing Street in 1988, she warned the prime minister that there would be no further meaningful reform, and certainly no release of Mandela, under PW Botha. We were going to have to work on his successors. When FW de Klerk emerged as the successor, she was cautiously optimistic, despite his conservative reputation, as she had always found him to be a decent and courteous person, uncontaminated by association with the coterie of securocrats clustered around PW Botha.

De Klerk then proceeded to surprise her, as he did

the world, by his readiness to take the steps she had advocated for so long, often using the same arguments she had deployed many times before. For, in January 1990, in a private meeting with senior officers of the South African Police, De Klerk told them that the only way to maintain the status quo was through an ever-increasing use of force, which he was not prepared to contemplate, and that, if this Armageddon took place, 'the problem will remain exactly the same as it was before the shooting started'.[2] On 2 February, he announced in parliament the unbanning of the ANC, the PAC and the South African Communist Party.

She had been vindicated, as had Johan Heyns, in the belief in the ultimate power of reason in persuading the government to change its course while there was time still to do so.

Chief Albert Luthuli had written to her in 1963: 'Not only ourselves – your contemporaries, but also posterity, will hold you in high esteem.' Greeting her in Tanzania, President Julius Nyerere said: 'Mrs Suzman, when all this is over, the role that you played will be remembered.'

It is important that it should be. For the success of the new South Africa will depend on the upholding in the future of the values that she and others fought for so valiantly in the darkest days of apartheid. As Nelson Mandela wrote of and for her: 'None can do more than her duty on earth ... you acquitted yourself beyond words.'

Appendix

Selected correspondence from the Helen Suzman papers, William Cullen Library, Wits University

replied 25/5/62.

A2084 MSI Luthuli, A. J.

Groutville Mission Reserve,
P.O. Groutville,
NATAL.

May, 18th. 1962.

Mrs. Helen Suzman, M.P.,
Houses of Parliament,
CAPE TOWN.

My Dear Mrs. Suzman,

Dr. Alan Paton, Dr. G.M. Naicker and I are
sponsoring a mass protest meeting in Durban on Friday, June 1, 1962.
The purpose of the meeting is to get the widest possible expression
of abhorence against the Sabotage Bill.

Ex Chief Justice van der Sandt Centlivres has
already been approached by me to be the main speaker. We would very
much like you to be one of the speakers as well.

Will you please give urgent consideration to this
request as time is running out and unless the greatest protest
against this inhuman Bill is voiced we shall undoubtedly find
South Africa in the throes of disorder and turmoil - a situation
we have done so much to avoid.

May I use this opportunity to congratulate you
on the gallant fight you are putting up, almost single-handed,
against Nationalist tyranny.

Looking forward to hearing from you and hoping
most sincerely that you will be able to address our meeting.

Yours sincerely,

A. J. LUTULI

Albert Luthuli (18 May 1962)

ALBERT JOHN LUTULI.

Groutville Mission,

P/Bag, P. O. Groutville.

6th May, 1963.

Dear Mrs. Suzman,

I take this opportunity to express my deep appreciation and admiration for your heroic and lone stand against a most reactionary Parliament, the Parliament of the Republic of the Union of South Africa. I most heartily congratulate you for your untiring efforts in a situation that would frustrate and benumb many.

In moments of creeping frustration and tiredness, please pick courage and strength in the fact, that thousands of South Africans, especially among the oppressed section, thank God for producing Helen, for her manly stand against injustice, regardless of consequences.

For ever remember, you are a bright Star in dark Chamber, where lights of liberty of what is left, are going out one by one.

This appreciation covers your contribution since you entered Parliament as member of the Progressive Party. This meritorious record has been climaxed by your fittingly uncompromising stand in the rape of democracy by Parliament in the debate that made law, which was one of the most diabolic bills, ever to come before Parliament.

Not only ourselves - your contemporaries, but also posterity, will hold you in high esteem.

Yours very truly,

"A. J. LUTULI"

Albert Luthuli (6 May 1963)

1338/88: NELSON MANDELA

Victor Verster Prison,
P/B X 6005,
Paarl South.
7624.
22 May 1989.

Dear Helen,

The consistency with which you defended the basic values of freedom and the rule of law over the last three decades has earned you the admiration of many South Africans.

A wide gap still exists between the mass democratic movement and your party with regard to the method of attaining those values. But your commitment to a non-racial democracy & a united South Africa has won you many friends in the extra-parliamentary movement.

Allow me to hope that you will continue to enjoy good health for years to come, that in the days that lie ahead your voice will be heard throughout the country, free from the restraints which parliamentary convention imposes.

Fondest regards and best wishes to you and your family.

Sincerely,
Nelson.

Nelson Mandela (22 May 1989)

LONG WALK TO FREEDOM

To my dearest Friend Helen,

Compliments and best wishes
to a redoubtable veteran of
many campaigns who has
contributed impressibly to
The victory of the democratic
forces of our Country

Mandela
23 · 1 · 95

Nelson Mandela (23 January 1995)

Message to Guests at
Helen Suzman's 85th Birthday Dinner
on 7 November 2002

We regret not being able to attend the birthday celebrations of another old die-hard veteran. Helen's resilience inspires us, convincing us that we are still quite young. It would have been a great pleasure to be present in order to thank her for the example she sets in how to advance with age without retreating.

Happy birthday, Helen. May this day be a joyful one, shared with friends and family who love and appreciate you. And may the year ahead and the years beyond be filled with joy and contentment and good health.

It needs not for us or anyone else to sing your praises: your place is ensured in the history of this country. Your courage, integrity and principled commitment to justice have marked you as one of the outstanding figures in the history of public life in South Africa.

On your 85th birthday, we can but pay tribute to you, thank you and let you know how fortunate our country feels for having had you as part of its public life and politics.

Now, looking back from the safety of our non-racial democracy, we can even feel some sympathy for the National Party members who shared Parliament with you. Knowing what a thorn in the flesh of even your friends and political allies you can be, your forthright fearlessness must have made life hell for them when confronted by you.

Helen, best wishes and thank you for being you. You are a very special person and South African.

NELSON MANDELA & GRAÇA MACHEL

7 November 2002

OUNCIL OF THE ELDERS

tribute to the veterans of the South African liberation struggle

To Helen,

Best wishes to a world-famous veteran freedom fighter who has earned enormous respect for beyond the borders of our Country.

Compiled and edited by
Firdoze Bulbulia
Faith Isiakpere

Mandela
27 · 9 · 98

MINAJ PUBLISHERS
LAGOS * LONDON * NEW YORK

Nelson Mandela (27 September 1998)

I

802 new Location,
Brandfort. O.F.S,
9400
20/11/79

Mrs Helen Suzman,
49 Melville Road,
Hyde Park
Sandton. 2199

Dearest Helen,

Your letter dated 12/11/79 has reached me
this minute and because I haven't heard
from you for a long time I could-n't resist the
temptation of pushing aside the impossible
correspondence I have which has accumulated
right through the year whilst I was preparing
for exams. Needless to tell you how much
I would have loved to see you.

I thank you for your continued concern
and am glad to note letters from you to me
are of interest to my guardians as well. Your
letter was very rudely opened and we
were not even favoured with the usual
crude courtesy of attempting to re-seal it.

If I had known before hand that you were
seeing Mr. Schlebush about me I would have
advised you not to bother about the aspect

Winnie Mandela (20 November 1979)

2

of my return to my house at this stage. I had similarly advised Mr Bizos in May this year when he felt it was time we raised this matter after he saw the state in which Zindzi is and the new problem I have to face of raising my grand-children in these deadly circumstances. Any human being would have compassion for the unnecessary cruelty we have been subjected to, particularly as they know the truth which is that if we had committed any crimes all the laws are there to have tried us. Having us in Brandfort is supposed to be the punishment of an ideal which we symbolise apparently, the name alone is a crime and the shooting of the ~~fists~~ at the mention of the name or by people who pass by the house was another reason for our exile I am told.

The reason why I would have advised you not to bother the Minister is because I have had a series of consultations with the present head of the security branch Brig. Johan Coetzee who saw me in this prison from February this year, on his last visit he was with General Geldenhuis. We

3

discussed several matters he had come to raise with me. I have known Brig. Coetzee for very many years and can assure you that I will be in Brandfort as long as he wishes me to remain in these circumstances and that no department of Justice can do anything for me at this stage. There are numerous other attempts he has made to help us and any type of help we have had has been from him. I shall not bore you with the details, some day they will be known.

We are trying to get a job though this is very complicated at this stage. As soon as I hear from those who are trying to help in this regard we shall renew our application for taking up the job otherwise I shall remain in this Brandfort prison for as long as they wish like all other prisoners who have no choice.

I hope for a period of rest during this Xmas, you deserve it after Edenvale, That was an achievement even if the situation remains the same.

Nelson sends his love, he is

recuperating well from the operation, I saw him on the 17th, that is last Saturday. He wishes me to go and receive the award from the Indian Government on his behalf, we shall once more make an application for a passport.

I hope it will not take very long to steam your letter open and that you will receive it before Xmas.

Fondest regards,
Winnie

802 New Location,
Brandfort. O.F.S.
9400.
I0.4.83

My dearest Helen,
Hearty congragulations for serving the people for the past twenty
years, it is a remarkable performance and gives one tremendous
inspiration and a lesson on perseviarance, I can assure you I am
taking notes.

Whilst you were away I visited Nelson and for the first time I
was distressed after a visit. There were many problems he raised
about Pollsmoor. His exact words were that it is now clear that
that the purpose of transferring them was further punishment, that
his treatment at present is what it was on Robben Island on their
arrival in I964.

He was distressed to learn you are still waiting for permission
to see him because he would have liked to discuss these problems
with you as a matter of urgency. He said to tell you that there
are now six of them in one cell as a result the following problems
have arisen :-

I.   They are not all studying, it is impossible to study whilst
the others are playing music and talking generally which they need
to do.

2.   Because of this he had been using an unoccupied cell next to
their cell. This he has been ordered to stop using.

3.   He then decided to study outside their cell or just infront
of it, he has been ordered never to do that again.

4.   When they requested that they be moved to single cells of the
same size they occupied on the Island, the prison authorities
simply divided one cell which is the size of the one they occupy at
present, they just put up partitions without any foundation and
they were threatening to move them to these isolation cells at the
end of the month. This he consideres most unhealthy and a danger
to their health.

5.   As he spoke he pointed to a pool of water which was behind
him, he said on the third floor where they are held the whole floor
is like that, water seeps through from beneath the cement floor even
when it is not raining. It had not rained that week-end I was in
Cape Town but the pool of water was there. He said on most mornings
when they wake up the floor is covered with water, that he would be
grateful if an inspection of this is done as a matter of urgency in
the interests of their health. By the way that was the only reason
why he was allowed to discuss this with me, he said he is allowed
to discuss his health with his family.

5.   He further stated that from their cell all they can see is the
sky, they are that confined, they are not allowed outside at alll
even for exercising, that is done inside, if ever they have to be
taken out such as when they are taken to the doctor the prison is
completely cleared, they are not to be seen by anybosy except the
officer who attends to them.

On the Island as you know they used to go outside and even take
walks around prison, now the last time they saw a blade of grass
was when they were moved from the Island.

Winnie Mandela (10 April 1983)

6. They are not allowed to buy sports attire, a question which was resolved years ago on the Island by the Red-Cross. As a result he had been using a wrong size shoe given by the prison for exercising when he developed the toe problem, the nail became black and he was examined by the specialist, he suggested that it should be removed and that is the operation he underwent.

The officer who is in charge of that is the same one who was in charge of their sports equipment on Robben Island. When they raised this with him he was most uncooperative.

7. When they realised that the situation is getting worse they asked to see the officer commanding and he refused to see them. They then asked if they could submit a memorundum to him and he refused to accept it, so at present they are unable to even complain.

8. They are no longer allowed to send or receive telegrams no matter how urgent a problem is, even if it is in connection with a death in the family.

He said I should tell you that the relationship between them and the warder who looks after them is fine and the food is much improved after a very bad start.

As you know you are the only one who can think of what wshould be done other their own courts. I am most distressed about this becaus Nelson never complains. It was the first time I heard him say how could he be expected to spend the rest of his life like that, and that their health is in grave danger.

I am sorry to welcome you back in this manner, as you say in the paper, you must really be very tired – veteran MP for LowereH! Why on earth don'nt you like that ? at least you cannot shoot me with the first shot, our friends are always around when you visit me, they are bound to protect me!

Thanks for the lovely short visit you paid me last time, it cheered me up a great deal.

Lots of love and fondest regards.

W Mandela

4,

802 New location,
Brandfort
O.F.S.
9400
25.8.84

Mrs. Helen Suzman,
49 Melville Road,
Hyde Park,
Sandton. 2199.

Dearest Helen,

Thank you so much for your letter which I received just now. As always I am extremely grateful for your very kind assistance even if you are going to have grave difficulties as usual in matters that affect me. M.K. was as usual found guilty on the 13th and sentenced to 90 days or R50. I expect them to re-arrest any day as they have been doing for the past four years until they learn you are doing something about it.

Thanks once more about bothering yourself with regard to the Hector P. Memorial lecture with all the work in your hands. It's highly appreciated.

Winnie Mandela (25 August 1984)

With regard to the Denmark prize
for us I wonder if it wouldn't be a
good idea to travel with my daughter
who is in Swaziland. Naturally I will
ask you to intervene & ask Pretoria
to issue me with a passport but
I know it's a fruitless exercise.

Would you also help me with the
purchase of the house you helped me
retreave from the state. I have
been trying to buy it, taking advantage
of the '99 year lease' thing surprising
with instructions from Nelson to do
so for the future of the children.
Ismail tells me they say I am not
in occupation of that house which
is utter nonsense. Please help us
buy it immediately to solve a lot
of problems.

I was also very upset to learn
you were disturbed by the report
conveyed to you by Bady on my
behalf with regard to Zindzi. I want
to explain that at that time, which was
the very morning, that was the
information conveyed to me by the
doctors at Baragwanath hospital. Like
any mother you can imagine how I
must have felt when I learnt of

the truth from the police in Johannesburg as Zindzi was unable to talk. I too learnt of the details from the press as I was sitting next to her daily at the hospital as she the fought for her life in intensive care. I want you to know I could never mislead you deliberately & subject you to any embarrassing situation knowingly.

Finally I took advantage of these friends to make sure the letter reaches you.

All my love & warmest regards to the family.

Forever yours

Winnie

We salute our dearest
friend Helen, one day
the nation will honour
your tremendous work.
You fight for our human
rights. You've always
been truly one of us
    Love
    Winnie Mandela

Winnie Mandela (1985)

Notes

Introduction

1 *Rand Daily Mail*, 20 Jan 1960.

2 Report-back, 25 June 1969.

3 Helen Suzman to author.

4 Helen Suzman, *In No Uncertain Terms*, Jonathan Ball, 1993, p. 114.

5 Suzman, *op. cit.*, pp. 68, 87; Hansard, 8 December 1978, col 519.

6 EJ Kahn, in *Values Alive – A Tribute to Helen Suzman*, Jonathan Ball, 1990, p. 171.

7 Examples given to the author by Helen Suzman. There were many more.

8 Irene Menell, in *Values Alive*, p. 2.

9 Helen Suzman papers, Historical Papers Research Archive, William Cullen Library, University of the Witwatersrand, Ba11.1, Di.

10 Hansard, 18 May 1989, col 9629.

Chapter I

1 Suzman papers, Ac1.2; Suzman, *op. cit.*, pp. 224-227; Donald Woods, *Asking for Trouble*, Victor Gollancz, 1980, pp. 304-12.

2 Suzman papers, Ad8.1-8.1.7, Am1.1; Suzman, *op. cit.*, pp. 227-230; Hansard, 12 May 1978, cols 6803-6804.

3 Suzman, *op. cit.*, p. 230; Suzman papers Ad8.1.6.

4 Suzman, *op. cit.*, pp. 205-6; Suzman papers, Ac1.3.

Chapter II

1 Suzman papers, 'The Reminiscences of Helen Suzman', Oral History, Columbia University, 1984, pp. 1-9, Ma7.1; Suzman, *op. cit.*, pp. 4-11; Suzman papers, Ma7.2, interview with David Welsh; Joanna Strangwayes-Booth (JSB), *A Cricket in the Thorn Tree: Helen Suzman and the Progressive Party*, Indiana University Press, 1976.

2 Suzman papers, Mb3.7.

3 *Star*, September 1949; JSB, *op. cit.*, p. 37.

4 Oral History, p. 11; Suzman, *op. cit.*, p. 14.

5 Suzman, *op. cit.*, p. 60.

6 Oral History, pp. 23, 26; Suzman, *op. cit.*, pp. 21-22.

7 Suzman, *op. cit.*, p. 48.

8 Hansard, 16 June 1955, cols 8044-5; JSB, *op. cit.*, p. 102.

9 Suzman papers, Aa1.2.9.

10 Report-back, 1954.

11 Hansard, 16 June 1955, cols 8044-5; JSB, *op. cit.*, p. 102.

12 *Rand Daily Mail*, 1 August 1957.

13 *Sunday Times* (Johannesburg), 16 October 1960.

14 Suzman papers, Ka6; JSB, *op. cit.*, p. 141.

15 Hansard, 10 April 1959, col 3424; Oral History, pp. 42-44.

16 JSB, *op. cit.*, p. 150.

17 Suzman, *op. cit.*, pp. 46-47; JSB, *op. cit.*, pp. 156-158.

Chapter III

1 Suzman, *op. cit.*, pp. 48-49; JSB, *op. cit.*, pp. 164, 169; *Rand Daily Mail*, 5 December 1959.

2 Suzman, *op. cit.*, p. 51; report-back, 1960.

3 Hansard, 30 March 1960, cols 4526-7.

4 Oral History, p. 133; Suzman, *op. cit.*, pp. 53-54.

5 Suzman, *op. cit.*, p. 68.

6 *Rand Daily Mail*, 16 September 1961; JSB, *op. cit.*, p. 193.

7 Hansard, 14 February 1961, cols 1309-10.

8 Suzman, *op. cit.*, p. 56.

9 Report-back, August 1962; Suzman, *op. cit.*, p. 89.

10 Report-back, 2 August 1962.

11 Hansard, 23 January 1963, col 108.

12 *Ibid.*

13 Hansard, 24 April 1963, col 4652.

14 Hansard, 24 April 1963, cols 4670-4680; report-back, 7 August 1963.

15 Suzman, *op. cit.*, p. 93; Suzman papers, Ma4.2.1.1 (emphasis in original).

16 *Natal Witness*, 30 May 1963.

17 Report-back, 7 August 1963.

18 Hansard, 25 February 1964, col 1962.

19 *Die Burger*, 7 March 1964; Hansard, 25 February 1964, cols 1953-4; David Welsh, in *Opposing Voices*, Jonathan Ball, 2006, p. 8.

20 Suzman papers, Mb2.4.2; report-back, 3 August 1965.

21 Suzman, *op. cit.*, p. 68.

22 *Sunday Times* (Johannesburg), 27 March 1966; *World*, 31 March 1966; *Post*, March 1966; *New York Times*, 1 April 1966.

23 Report-back, 5 November 1966.

24 Suzman papers, Mb2.5.1; Oral History, pp. 54-58; Suzman, *op. cit.*, pp. 69-71.

Chapter IV

1 Suzman papers, Ka3.

2 Suzman, *op. cit.*, pp. 72-73; Oral History, p. 135; Suzman papers, Mb2.5.1.

3 Suzman, *op. cit.*, p. 82; Re Mandela, Helen Suzman to the author; see also Anthony Sampson, *Mandela*, Harper Press, 1999, p. 454.

4 Suzman papers, Mb2.3.1.

5 Suzman papers, Ld, Mb2.3.1 and 2.3.2; Suzman, *op. cit.*, pp. 76-77.

6 Hansard, 1 June 1967, cols 7039-7047; Hansard, 2 June 1967, col 7114; Suzman, *op. cit.*, pp. 97-98.

7 Hansard, 23 April 1968, cols 3936-39, and 6 June 1968, cols 6669 and 6679.

8 Suzman papers, Hc8.1, Mb2.13.1.

9 Report-back, 25 June 1969.

10 Suzman, *op. cit.*, p. 114.

11 Suzman, *op. cit.*, p. 115.

12 Suzman, *op. cit.*, pp. 116-17, 119-20; Suzman papers, Aa1.2.9, Ma10.8, Mb1.

13 Suzman, *op. cit.*, pp. 120-22; Donald Woods, *op. cit.*, p. 150.

14 Report-back, 1 November 1966.

15 Report-back, August 1968.

16 Suzman papers, tribute from Alan Paton, Ma8.4.1.

17 Hansard, 21 April 1969, cols 4433-6, and 22 July 1970, cols 201-12; Suzman, *op. cit.*, pp. 124-25.

18 Hansard, 21 April 1969, cols 4433-6.

19 *Die Vaderland*, 28 November 1969; JSB, *op. cit.*, p. 235.

20 Suzman, *op. cit.*, p. 294.

21 Suzman papers, Mb 2.9.1; Suzman, *op. cit.*, pp. 125-26.

22 Hansard, 6 May 1971, col 5950; JSB, *op. cit.*, p. 128.

23 Hansard, 3 February 1971, col 227; Suzman, *op. cit.*, p. 78.

24 Suzman papers, Mb2.9.1.

25 Suzman, *op. cit.*, p. 128.

26 Hansard, 11 March 1971, cols 2513-4.

27 Report-back, 21 June 1972.

28 Oral History, pp. 63-65; Hansard, 26 April 1972, cols 5828 and 5830; Suzman, *op. cit.*, pp. 86-87.

29 JSB, *op. cit.*, p. 246.

30 *Rand Daily Mail*, 28 February 1973; Hansard, 8 March 1973, col 2265.

31 Oral History, p. 63; Suzman, *op. cit.*, p. 132.

32 Helen Zille, in *Opposing Voices, op. cit.*, p. 97.

33 Hansard, 23 September 1970, cols 4830-4838.

34 Suzman papers, Ma8.4.2; Suzman, *op. cit.*, p. 133.

Chapter V

1 Breyten Breytenbach, *The True Confessions of an Albino Terrorist*, Taurus, 1984, p. 102.

2 Nelson Mandela, foreword to *In No Uncertain Terms*, p. ix.

3 Suzman, *op. cit.*, pp. 142-45; Suzman papers, Ma3.1.2.3; Oral History, pp. 143, 146-48.

4 Suzman papers, Ab1.3.

5 Suzman papers, Aa4.1, Ab5.1; Suzman, *op. cit.*, pp. 152-54, 220-21; Oral History, pp. 139-41.

6 Neville Alexander, in *Values Alive*, p. 67; Suzman papers, Aa1.2.1.

7 Suzman papers, Mb2.13.2.

8 Suzman, *op. cit.*, pp. 154-56; Nelson Mandela, foreword to *In No Uncertain Terms*, p. x; Suzman papers, Aa4.2; Oral History, p. 157.

9 Suzman papers, Aa1.2.6; Suzman, *op. cit.*, pp. 155-56.

10 Suzman papers, Ad1.3.1.

11 Suzman papers, Ab5.2, Mc1.19, Mc1.27; Suzman, *op. cit.*, pp. 156-57; *International Herald Tribune*, 4 July 1983.

12 Suzman papers, Ab5.2; Suzman, *op. cit.*, pp. 157-58.

13 Suzman, *op. cit.*, p. 163.

14 Oral History, pp. 47-48; Suzman papers, Mc1.17.

15 Suzman papers, Ab3.4.1 and 3.4.2; Suzman, *op. cit.*, p. 166.

16 Suzman papers, Mb3.4.2, Mb2.22.1; Suzman, *op. cit.*, pp. 165-69.

17 Suzman, *op. cit.*, p. 167; Suzman papers, Mb3.4.

18 Family papers.

19 Suzman, *op. cit.*, pp. 168-69.

20 Family papers.

Chapter VI

1 Suzman, *op. cit.*, pp. 174, 191.

2 Suzman, *op. cit.*, p. 182.

3 Suzman papers, Mb3.2.

4 Suzman papers, Jb3, Mb2.16.1.

5 Suzman, *op. cit.*, pp. 185-86.

6 Suzman, *op. cit.*, pp. 220-23; Suzman papers, on Robert

Sobukwe, Ab1.1, Ab3, Bb5, Mb2.3.2, Mb2.8.1 and Mb2.17.1; Oral History, pp. 187-90.

7   Suzman papers, La4.2.

8   Suzman papers, Md2.

9   Hansard, 18 May 1965, col 6243; Suzman, *op. cit.*, pp. 83-84.

10 Hansard, 8 December 1978, col 519.

11 Hansard, 6 February 1980, col 240; Suzman papers, Lh, Mb2.19.1.

12 Suzman papers, Aa1.2.6, Ad8.2, Md3; Suzman, *op. cit.*, pp. 232-37.

13 Hansard, 25 August 1981, col 1921.

14 Hansard, 26 February 1985, col 1421.

15 Suzman, *op. cit.*, p. 216.

16 Suzman papers, Aa1.2.9.

17 Suzman papers, De2.

18 Suzman, *op. cit.*, p. 190.

Chapter VII

1   Suzman, *op. cit.*, p. 246.

2   Hansard, 14 March 1985, col 2283.

3   Hansard, 16 June 1986, col 8423.

4   Suzman papers, Aa1.2.2, Ai.

5   Suzman papers, Ad1.4, Mb2.23.2, Mb2.24.1.

6   Suzman papers, Mb2.24.1.

7   Suzman papers, Mb2.26.1.

8 Suzman, *op. cit.*, p. 254.

9 Suzman papers, Gb1.

10 Colin Eglin, *Crossing the Borders of Power*, Jonathan Ball, 2007, pp. 243-45; Suzman papers, Af9.

11 Suzman papers, Jb1.1.

12 Suzman papers, Mb2.28.1.

13 Suzman papers, Fb3, Fd; Suzman, *op. cit.*, pp. 257-59.

14 Suzman papers, Mb.4.

15 Suzman papers, Mb2.9.1, 2.10.1, Mb2.

16 Suzman papers, La4.1; Oral History, pp. 206-209.

17 Suzman papers, Je, La4 and Ma8.4.2.

Chapter VIII

1 Suzman, *op. cit.*, pp. 276-77.

2 Suzman, *op. cit.*, pp. 277-78; Suzman papers, Ma3 1.2.3.

3 Hansard, 18 May 1989, col 9626.

4 Suzman papers, Ae6.1, 6.2 and 6.3; Hansard, 23 May 1989, cols 10013 *et seq.*; Suzman, *op. cit.*, pp. 279-81.

5 Suzman papers, Ma8.2.1; Suzman, *op. cit.*, p. 275.

6 Handwritten letter of 19 May 1989 from Helen Suzman to Prime Minister Margaret Thatcher. Family papers.

7 Suzman papers, Ab5.1, Mb8.2; Suzman, *op. cit.*, pp. 163-64.

8 Suzman papers, Mb2.28.1.

9 Anthony Sampson, *op. cit.*, p. 223; Suzman papers, Mb1.

10 Suzman papers, Aj2; Nadine Gordimer, in *Values Alive*, p. 118.

Chapter IX

1 *Washington Post*, June 1990.

2 Suzman papers, Ke2.1; Suzman, *op. cit.*, pp. 283-84.

3 Suzman papers, speech to SAIRR, Mj1.1.

4 Sampson, *op. cit.*, pp. 434, 456.

5 Suzman papers, Ma10.1.

6 Eglin, *op. cit.*, p. 99.

7 Family papers.

8 Suzman papers, Ls, Mb3.1, 3.2 and 3.3.

9 Helen Suzman to the author.

10 Oral History, p. 99.

11 Suzman papers, Mb3.5.

12 Interview with Bobby Godsell in *Optima*, May 2004.

13 Ronald Suresh Roberts, *Fit to Govern: The Native Intelligence of Thabo Mbeki*, STE, 2007, p. 30; Suzman papers, Mb3.7.

14 Suzman papers, Hc8.1.

Chapter X

1 *Focus*, Journal of the Helen Suzman Foundation, April 2009.

2 Speech by FW de Klerk at the Police College, Pretoria, 10 January 1990; Robin Renwick, *Unconventional Diplomacy in Southern Africa*, Macmillan, 1997, p. 139; Hermann Giliomee, *The Last Afri-kaner Leaders*, Tafelberg, 2012, pp. 304-305.

Acknowledgements

I am extremely grateful to Helen Suzman's family, especially to her daughter Dr Frances Jowell for kindly giving me access to all of Helen Suzman's private papers, held in the Historical Papers Research Archive, William Cullen Library, at the University of the Witwatersrand, and for her and their comments on the manuscript. My warmest thanks are due to Ruth Muller, for her excellent catalogue of the papers and for invaluable help in enabling me to access them, and to Michele Pickover at the William Cullen Library. Thanks to a grant from the Oppenheimer Memorial Trust, the papers will be digitised, facilitating access for future authorised researchers.

No one writing about Helen Suzman can fail to place considerable reliance on her autobiography, published in 1993 by Jonathan Ball and characteristically entitled *In No Uncertain Terms*. I hope that this book will encourage others to read or reread it. A valuable and detailed history of her career up to 1975, *A Cricket in the Thorn Tree*, written by Joanna Strangwayes-Booth, was published by Indiana University Press in 1976. *Helen Suzman's Solo Years*, edited by Dr Phyllis Lewsen, published by Jonathan Ball in 1975, is another valuable resource.

Other important contributions about her are to be found in the oral history 'Reminiscences of Helen Suzman', which she dictated in 1984 for Columbia University, as well as in *Values Alive – A Tribute to Helen Suzman*, published by Jonathan Ball in 1990; *Helen Suzman – Fighter for Human Rights*, published by the Kaplan Centre at the University of Cape Town in 2005; the Helen Suzman Foundation Tribute Edition of *Focus*, April 2009; and Gillian Godsell's excellent study for schoolchildren, *Helen Suzman*, published by Maskew Miller Longman in 2011.

I am also grateful to David Welsh, Ruth Muller, Irene Menell, John Battersby, Stanley Uys and Ann Bernstein for kindly giving me their comments on the manuscript, and to Daniel Jowell for his help in accessing additional documents.

My thanks are due to Ruth Muller and Marie-France Renwick for their help in sourcing the photographs, and to Katie Gareh for her invaluable assistance.

In my time as the British ambassador to South Africa in the years preceding and immediately following Nelson Mandela's release from prison, Helen Suzman was my closest friend and greatest ally. Much of the latter part of this account is based on my own experiences of and innumerable conversations with her and with her colleagues, especially Van Zyl Slabbert and Colin Eglin. Where any quotation is not attributed, it was verified with her.

Index

219

Index

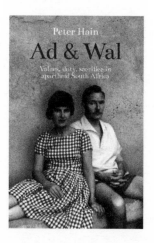